When we aren't in class, doing hom
playing sports, or helping out at the
boba shop.

M000278065

The boba shop isn't easy to get to. But we go, because it's our place.

It's a forty-minute ride in a friend's old van from South San Francisco High School to Wonderful Foods in the Richmond District.

It's tucked away in a strip mall on Bellaire, in Houston, where we take Sunday afternoon Mandarin classes, next to that arcade where kids smoke cigarettes and make out.

It's a bunch of teenagers crowded in front of a storefront in a San Gabriel parking lot after school lets out.

Mom hardly ever gives us money but she does for the boba shop, where the drinks are sweet and chewy. She knows if we're at the boba shop, we aren't at home playing StarCraft or out doing anything else we shouldn't be.

The boba shop is in the Asian part of town but we always take our non-Asian friends there. They love it. And while we don't always see many kids that look like us at school, we see them at the boba shop.

We're kids. We don't know much about where we're from. But we do know boba is from Asia. (In fact, it's from Taiwan, the place our families left behind to raise us in America.)

But that's there, and we're here. So Asia doesn't feel like our place. And to be honest, a lot of the time America doesn't feel like our place, either. But the boba shop does.

And the boba shop is a little bit of both places. Kinda like us.

We are the Boba Generation.

THE BOBA BOOK

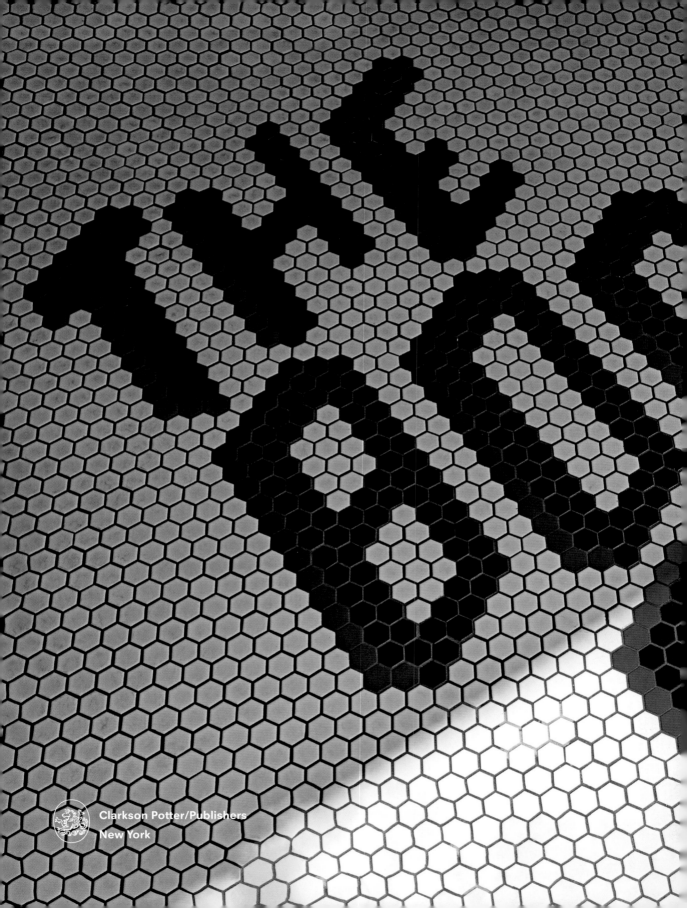

Clarkson Potter/Publishers
New York

Bubble Tea & Beyond

Andrew Chau and Bin Chen,
aka the Boba Guys

With Richard Parks III

**Photographs by
Christopher Testani**

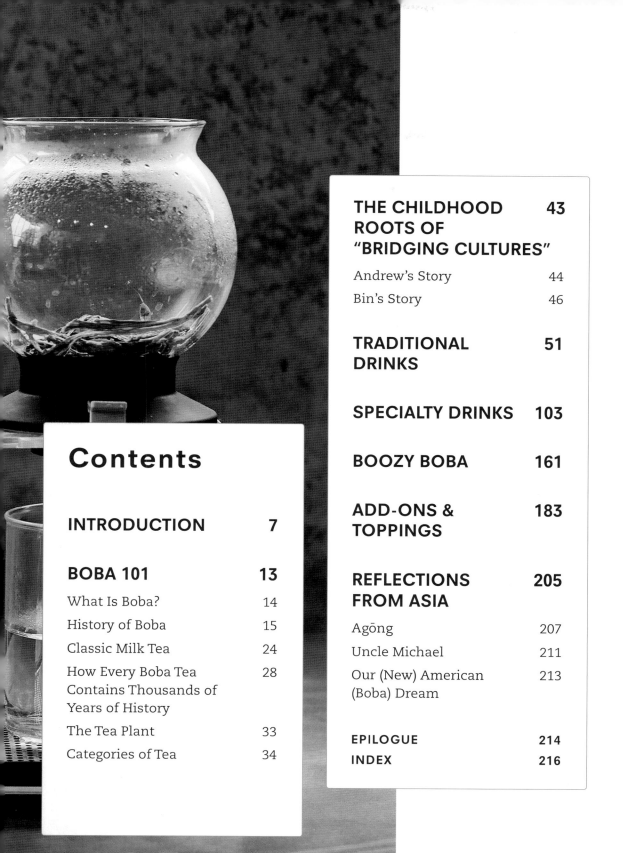

Contents

INTRODUCTION   7

BOBA 101   13

What Is Boba?   14

History of Boba   15

Classic Milk Tea   24

How Every Boba Tea   28
Contains Thousands of
Years of History

The Tea Plant   33

Categories of Tea   34

THE CHILDHOOD   **43**
ROOTS OF
"BRIDGING CULTURES"

Andrew's Story   44

Bin's Story   46

TRADITIONAL   **51**
DRINKS

SPECIALTY DRINKS   **103**

BOOZY BOBA   **161**

ADD-ONS &   **183**
TOPPINGS

REFLECTIONS   **205**
FROM ASIA

Agōng   207

Uncle Michael   211

Our (New) American   213
(Boba) Dream

EPILOGUE   **214**

INDEX   **216**

INTRODUCTION

It's 95 degrees plus humidity, the trees are screaming with cicadas, and buses packed with Chinese tourists peering out from lace-curtain-covered windows are lumbering through the intersections. Scooters whiz past at nerve-racking speeds. We're a long way from San Francisco. And it smells like stinky tofu, because Taipei always smells like stinky tofu.

But we're not here for stinky tofu. We're here at Chen San Ding for the chewy tapioca balls known as *boba*. (No, they're not "blobs.") The batch we've got in our hands comes swimming in deep brown syrup at the bottom of a 16-ounce plastic cup; a pour of ice-cold milk on top means beads of condensation start forming instantly. A few brisk stirs of a wide straw send dark plumes upward through the thick, malty milk, and the drink ranges from white to deep brown and beige.

Soft, warm boba zip up the straw along with the deep caramelized flavor of the syrupy milk, rich like heavy cream. It's like a drinkable crème brûlée, or flan—but it's liquid and chewy all at once. The tapioca is firm, dense, and bouncy; the Taiwanese call the texture *QQ*.

It's perfect. The best thing we'll taste that day.

But to us, boba is much more than a drink. It's like American apple pie or Beyoncé's *Lemonade*. There's the thing itself, and all the lore and backstory to go with it, too. Not to over-romanticize a simple drink, but boba is an experience—about history, culture, and identity. And if you look hard enough into that cloudy cup, you'll probably learn something about Asia, about America, and, we think, about our society's future.

Like most Asian Americans our age, we first encountered boba as kids. It was the early '90s and boba was fresh off the boat from Taiwan, the place our parents had left behind to raise us here in the U.S. We loved everything about it. It was creamy, sweet, colorful—what's not to like? And it was playful. We loved using the oversize straw to suck up the chewy tapioca

> I remember when boba showed up in L.A. in the '90s as a fad.

> Well, we wouldn't call it a fad since it's an Asian staple. But we know it's new for a lot of people. Just think of it like how you think of a Frappuccino!

lying at the bottom of the cup. The best of us could finish both the tapioca and liquid part of the beverage at the exact same time. It's a skill. As the lone Asian kids at our respective suburban American schools, this was *our* thing. It made us feel like we had something to call our own, but we also wanted to share it with the rest of the world. It's like having the salted caramel ice cream from Bi-Rite Creamery and never shutting up about it. OK, we're Asian, so we kinda did shut up about it . . . until now.

As we've grown up, we've realized that boba remains a bridge between the two cultures we come from. It's from Taiwan, after which it spread to Japan and China and throughout Asia, but it's also here to stay in New York, San Francisco, L.A., Chicago, Houston, Atlanta, and your local neighborhood. The food Medici give all the love to the finer things like coffee, wine, and chocolate. But where's the love? For every Blue Bottle, Momofuku, or Starbucks, there is a boba shop that is changing the way Americans consume beverages.

At our Boba Guys stores, we represent, but also reinterpret the sweet after-school drink of our childhoods. Our Classic Milk Tea (page 24) captures the essence of our beloved childhood boba. But we're also known for our Strawberry Matcha Latte (page 104), which is delicious and, OK, looks sexy on

> The working subtitle for this book was *"How to Save the World from WWIII."*
>
> It really was a little too much.

Instagram, like a tricolor Rothko with polka dots. Or the "Dirty" Horchata (page 150), a coffee-fueled riff on the rice-milk-and-cinnamon drink we fell for at the taquerias in our neighborhood. We're trying to expand the definition of what boba is, for everybody.

On any given afternoon at our Mission District location you'll find a 60-year-old *abuelita* crushing a "Dirty" Horchata with boba next to a stylish 30-something Everlane-wearing mom sipping one of our colorful seasonal tea frescas, her toddler wandering around with a strawberry rice milk and bumping into a Supreme-dripping Hypebeast sucking down a Classic Milk Tea. We have a drink in our stores for just about everyone, and in this book, we'll show you how to make them all, with recipes as diverse as our community. It's all about bridging cultures, our mission since coming out as a pop-up in 2011. Coffee had its revolution over a decade ago. We started one for boba.

Boba started in Asia, came to America, and is being remixed and repackaged in a way that can speak to both old and new generations. It's like the Rihanna song "FourFiveSeconds" with Kanye. And Paul McCartney. In a black and white music video. It's the best of every world. We're culturally wildin'. That's what we Americans do best, right? It's the American Future.

—Andrew and Bin
aka the Boba Guys

Our first store in the Mission District of San Francisco, where it all began.

The Feng Chia Night Market in Taichung, Taiwan. Known as the largest night market in Taiwan and home to countless drinks stalls.

Bridging Cultural Operating Systems

You might have seen the text bubbles floating around this book. Let us explain.

"Hey, Richard, it's Andrew."

"Old phone, who dis?"

We love seeing green text bubbles on our iPhones. A green text is like, "You have a friend with an Android phone!" About 80 percent of our friends have iPhones, so it's just nice to know that friendships cross operating systems.

Richard Parks III, our cowriter for this book, is our green text bubble in real life. There's nobody more old-school American than Richard. His family has been here since before the Revolutionary War. (That was a long time ago.)

When we were looking for a writer, we searched far and wide for the ~~white~~ right voice to pair with our Asian-ness. This is a book about drinks, but really it's a book about bridging cultures. We wanted someone who could help us broaden our perspective. And if we picked another Asian writer, well, you'd probably assume this was FABA: *For Asians, By Asians*. But this book is for everyone. (OK, let's get real. Y'all know Asians just want one person to approve of this book . . . our moms! They both signed up for ten first-run copies.)

They just need to be hot! And the dough needs to be cooked. And there needs to be hot liquid inside.

So any writer we worked with had to get it. We even took Richard to Asia with us, where he got a crash course in everything Asian. Like *everything*. He was already a self-proclaimed "*xiao long bao* snob."

LOL it was only one word, repeated three times: *Búyào búyào búyào!*

We knew we'd made the right choice when we saw him use the only three Mandarin words he knew to get a hat down to half price in Taipei.

And now you have a hat with "DON'T PRAY FOR LOVE" written on the front

But there's still a disconnect. We feel that disconnect sometimes. We felt it when Richard had trouble fitting his size 11 feet into the wooden *yukata* slippers you wear at a Japanese hot spring. We feel it when we take him to boba shops and notice how he conspicuously always passes on the cendol. Richard Parks III is our green text bubble.

I love it! It's hanging on the wall in my office. Hopefully some of that hat's magic will work its way into the book!

But even with that disconnect, he can still text us. We can read each other's messages. We can even send emojis back and forth. We're still talking, bridging cultures, even across different operating systems. There's a great C++ joke in here, but our very expensive professional writer edited it out. *Cue "It's a Small World" theme music.

BOBA 101

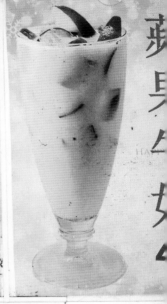

There's never been a book about boba from a mainstream Western publisher. You're reading the first one. When we started selling boba at a pop-up in 2011, we pulled what we could from blogs and YouTube videos to make our first drinks, like the classic milk tea. But as we grew and experimented with our own increasingly ambitious boba creations, we knew that there had to be a book one day—and we knew we could write it.

It's for boba lovers and boba newbies alike. While this book is littered with boba culture references, we want it to feel at home in any café (not just boba shop) in America.

This chapter gives you the brass tacks, the 4-1-1, the essential lowdown on what you need to know—and what we wish we could have found in a book when we first started out.

What Is Boba?

Hi! I'm a cup of boba, also known as "bubble tea." I'm a sweet and creamy mix of milk and tea. You drink me with a big straw that you also use to suck up tapioca balls, a.k.a. "boba," that are dark and chewy. So I'm a drink that you can chew. I was born in Taiwan in the mid-1980s. (So I'm technically a millennial!) But now I live all over the world. And these days, there are thousands of variations on me: different teas and flavors, milk alternatives, fruit, and different toppings in place of and in addition to boba. The possibilities are kind of endless. The guys who wrote this book are going tell you a lot more. But I wanted to jump in and say hi first. Hi! This is me in my most-classic state. Hope you enjoy getting to know me and my story.

Straw

Milk

Tea

Boba

History of Boba

Who made the first cup of boba?

We don't know that anyone truly knows.

This is what we can all agree on: Boba represents thousands of years of history and culture-bridging stirred together into a single drink. You take a classical tea preparation from ancient China and India, add milk and sugar in the 18th-century European tradition, and drop in tapioca balls, made from a root native to Brazil but popularized in snow ice desserts in 1980s Taiwan. So we can also pretty much agree that it was in Taiwan that someone put all that history into a single cup.

The rub lies in this next part, the competing origin stories of *where* the OG boba milk tea was first served in the 1980s. Was it Chun Shui Tang, the venerable Taichung-based restaurant chain? Or was it Hanlin Tea Room, in Tainan? We've been in the boba business for almost a decade, so we thought we could be Sir Walter Raleigh on the expedition to find El Dorado . . . the DJ Kool Herc of boba milk tea.

We started by visiting the original Chun Shui Tang on a hot, humid July afternoon.

CST, founded in 1983, feels more like a Western-style restaurant than most of Asia's current drinks hot spots, which are mostly busy street stalls or in malls. At 2 p.m., it's packed with families seated in wooden booths beneath decorative lanterns, the tables crowded with teas. It smells like a spa (in a good way). The CST menu claims it to be "the creator of pearl milk tea," which is OK, but also "the origin of handmade drinks," which seems . . . dubious?

As we sat there, nursing our teas in large milkshake glasses, we tried to email Hanlin Tea Room's representatives. We couldn't wait to crack the case, like two Encyclopedia ~~Browns~~ Yellows.

Eventually a CST representative, Yu Ching Wu, sat with us. Clean bob, neatly tucked blouse—she was ready for business.

After a half hour of pleasantries and guanxi (the Chinese word for building relationships), we finally took a breath and went for it: "Do you really think you invented boba milk tea?"

Yu Ching Wu dodged the question of whether CST actually invented boba milk tea . . . again and again. She talked about how they were inspired by seeing people in Japan putting ice in coffee back in 1983, then decided to try it with their milk tea. OK, so we have the story of the *cold* part of the drink . . . was this going to take forever? "But what about the balls??" we asked, desperate for the truth. We almost slammed the table like Tom Cruise in *A Few Good Men*.

And this is when the world parted. It's like that moment when Snoop Dogg's voice pops into "California Gurls" with Katy Perry. We had to rewind this part of the conversation over and over.

"I don't know," she said. "And we don't really care."

As the kids say, we were shook.

> Is that too many references in one sentence?
>
> I don't know, let's ask our editor.
>
> Well, he says he thought Walter Raleigh was the first English dude to show up in Hawai'i, so he has no clue.

She explained: Maybe they did it first, maybe Hanlin Tea Room did it first. But what mattered to them was that CST made it popular. They took it global. In the sweetest Asian gangster tone, she said, "This is how we see food. It's about consistency and doing it best, not about who did it first."

We'd come all this way for an interview with the supposed inventor of boba milk tea, only to find out that they didn't care if they were the inventor of boba milk tea! Sure, they had their story about that very first cup of boba milk tea, and they knew that Hanlin Tea Room did, too. But fundamentally, they didn't care about proving they were right about being first, because they knew they were the ones that did it best.

In that moment, we realized something crucial: Maybe being Run-DMC is better than being DJ Kool Herc. The perfector, the next-leveler, may be more important than the originator.

> Can we think of someone who'd fit the Run DMC/Kool Herc analogy? LOL, MC Jin??

> Jin seems right!

> Who is MC Jin?

> Only the most-famous Asian rapper of all time!

> There were definitely ones that came before him, but he is the icon. He's in the Freestyle Friday Hall of Fame on 106 & Park!

> Namaste.

Chi Ku

When we relistened to the audio of our interview with Yu Ching Wu, we found ourselves embarrassed. Stephanie Tanner should have been there, saying, "How rude!"

Asian culture typically values delayed gratification a bit more than American culture. The concept of guanxi relies on a long-term approach to building relationships, not just transactions. And so listening to our very direct questions, we realized we sounded a bit aggressive in context, even if in America we would be described as just "cutting to the chase."

In the Chinese language, it is often said one must "chi ku," which translates to "eat bitter." It basically means to do what's hard now (like eating bitter melon or food), so you can benefit later (because bitter food is good for you). In Taiwan, if you watch people park their cars, you'll see people usually reverse into their parking spots, and then when they leave, they drive out easily, facing forward—they get the hard stuff out of the way first.

We recommend the book *The Culture Map* by Erin Meyer if you find any of this remotely interesting.

What's Up With the Name "Boba"?

"Boba" refers to those little chewy, dark tapioca balls you'll see in our drinks. It can be singular or plural, like many of our favorite words.

"Sheep"

"Pants"

"Smithereens"

But when we say "boba" in this book, we're often talking about the whole drink, not just the balls. As in, "Let's go grab boba after work." That's how we grew up using the word. And boba doesn't necessarily *have* to have tapioca pearls in it—it could be a different topping, or even no topping. (Yes, the word "topping" is also confusing because they tend to sink to the bottom, but what are you going to call them, "fillings?") The Mandarin phrase *yin liao*, which translates as "beverages," is kind of analogous to how we use "boba" in this way.

But what's the difference between "boba" and "bubble tea"?

Ah, good question. If you live on the East Coast or in Canada, you might know "boba" as "bubble tea." We don't use this term because the "bubble" in "bubble tea" originally referred to the bubbles on the top of the drink that you get from shaking it up. But then people started calling the tapioca pearls "bubbles." We don't hate it, but we're kinda stuck with our name and we invested a lot of IP protection money into it, so we'll go with "boba."

And speaking of being stuck with our name . . . there's a whole other layer to this.

You guys love your layers!

ANDREW: My mom's Taiwanese, right? So when I told my mom I was starting a company called Boba Guys, I thought she'd be proud that I was promoting something from her native country. But "Andrew, *Boba* Guys?!" she screamed at me over the phone. "*Boba Guys??*"

I had no idea what she was upset about. But it turns out that back in the 1980s and '90s, "boba" was Taiwanese slang for "big *boobs*." There was even a whole fan culture around large-chested female actresses called "boba girls."

But we'd already designed our logo and brand ID. We were beyond the point of no return for the name. We were the Boobs Guys. I had no idea. And it was only while we were writing this book that I finally got to ask Bin, "Hey, when did you know what it meant in slang?"

BIN: Oh, I knew the whole time. Since I was a kid.

ANDREW: Dude, way to leave me hanging with my mom! Thankfully it's a little outdated as slang at this point and in Taiwan, *boba* is now commonly known as *zhenzhu*—"pearls."

The Boba Book

The Drinks You'll Find in a Boba Shop

Milk Teas (奶茶)

Milk and tea and tapioca balls are the staple flavor combo in almost every boba shop in the world. It was popularized by the Taiwanese chains Hanlin Tea Room and Chun Shui Tang, and it proliferated across Taiwan in the 1980s and '90s. The basic milk teas are traditional staple teas such as black tea, green tea, or even oolongs.

Lattes (拿铁)

A subset of milk teas, with the most notable difference being the ratio of milk to tea. Lattes, as the name would suggest, are mostly milk. They often take the form of matcha lattes in boba shops, although more shops in the U.S. are bringing other traditional Asian ingredients over to flavor these drinks. Sometimes in this book we use "latte" to refer to trending café drinks that are more akin to what you might know as a smoothie. (See Global Café Speak, page 87.) You'll see Ube Lattes, Sweet Potato Lattes, and Red Bean Lattes in this category.

Traditional Teas (茶)

Most boba shops do see themselves as tea shops, so you'll often see several varieties of tea, like High Mountain Oolong, Red Jade a.k.a. Ruby 18, or Ceylon tea, freshly brewed, on the menu. These differ from normal iced teas in American cafés in that these teas are usually more specialized. You don't see a lot of boba shops selling straight English breakfast hot tea.

Fruit Teas (水果茶)

A bit of a fruit tea renaissance has been emerging across all boba shops. Historically, fruit teas were flavored with syrups, but recently more boba shops are raising the quality of an average drink, so we now see natural fruit paired with a tea base, such as a jasmine or light oolong tea.

Crème Brûlée Teas / Cake Teas / Cheese Teas

This is an emerging style of milk tea featuring a rich topping that is a cross between whipped cream and buttercream spread. It's often made with cream cheese, so some of the drinks are called "cheese teas." Derivatives now include Crème Brûlée Teas and "Cake" Teas, which use an even thicker milk topping. You enjoy these drinks by sipping on the tea through the bottom of the straw while poking around for creamy pockets that slowly mix into the tea.

CLASSIC MILK TEA

This is what started everything. Take what is basically a simple British milk tea and put a Taiwanese dessert into it. Nothing fancy. But it's unmistakable. The classic combination of sweetened black tea, milk, and tapioca balls is the very definition of bridging cultures with a drink.

However much you tweak it with different syrups, milks, or teas, you just hear that same beat underneath and you know what it is.

It's like Queen and David Bowie's "Under Pressure." It's in "Ice Ice Baby" and a million other songs, but no matter who's spitting rhymes, you'd never mistake it for something else.

Like that sample, you'll hear this basic beat throughout the recipes in this book.

MAKES 1 GLASS

RECOMMENDED TOPPINGS: BOBA, COCONUT ALMOND JELLY, GRASS JELLY

2 to 4 tablespoons toppings of your choice (optional)

5 ounces (by weight) ice cubes

2 ounces House Syrup (page 27), or to taste

1 cup Brewed Boba Guys' Black Tea (page 27)

2½ ounces (¼ cup + 1 tablespoon) half-and-half (or oat milk, almond milk, soy milk, etc.) (See note.)

Fill a glass with the toppings, if using, and the ice, and then add the syrup. Pour the tea over the ice. Add the half-and-half. Stir until everything is mixed.

NOTE:

We use half-and-half in our default recipe because it gives the drink a creamy body. It's the closest creaminess to non-dairy creamer, which is what many boba shops actually use, and the flavor we grew up with. The half-and-half also counters the strong tea base. You can substitute with whole milk or non-dairy alternative milks, but you'll likely need a less potent tea base to get the same balance. We prefer oat milk as the dairy alternative as it's creamier than almond, coconut, and soy milks and it offers the same balance as half-and-half in our recipe.

Boba Guys' Tea Blend

These days, we have an in-house product team. But back when we started out as a pop-up, we were just a couple of tea nerds in corporate America. We came at boba from a world of iterative improvement and the scientific method. We pulled on our lab coats, set up our laptops, fired up Microsoft Excel, and started testing all the possible combinations of black teas that would make the perfect base for a classic boba. It was a jittery few weeks, but we finally landed on the perfect combination: mellow and round, slightly astringent, and fiercely strong. It's delicious and zippy, and powerful enough to stand up to the milk and sweetness. It has never changed since that first pop-up.

Assam is the maltiest of the famous black teas. It has a very smooth tea taste to it, but it's a little mellow on its own. The reason we use Ceylon, which is from Sri Lanka, is that it has more of the tannic quality that you associate with tea and adds a punch the Assam doesn't bring. Ceylon is also the most popular variety for traditional milk teas. Yunnan teas tend to be a little smokier. This gives our black tea blend a complexity that we just love.

MAKES 1 CUP, ENOUGH FOR 8 SERVINGS

½ cup Assam black tea leaves
¼ cup Ceylon black tea leaves
¼ cup Yunnan black tea leaves

Combine the tea leaves in a mixing bowl; stir well to fully mix. Store in an airtight container.

NOTE:

You'll notice, most of the drinks recipes in this book are broken into different components. That's because we encourage you to mix and match to create your own drinks!

Brewed Boba Guys' Black Tea

MAKES 1 GLASS

4 ounces (by weight) ice cubes

2 tablespoons Boba Guys' Tea Blend (recipe opposite)

5 ounces filtered water, heated to 190°F

Fill a tall glass with the ice cubes. Steep the tea leaves in the water for 4 minutes. Strain the tea over the ice, and set the glass aside to allow the ice to fully melt.

Since this makes such a large quantity, could I use this in my morning coffee, in cocktails, etc.?

Of course!

House Syrup

In bartending, there are many concentrates and flavorings. We get a little nerdy with infusions in syrups, like infusing rose leaves (see Rose Syrup, page 121) and spirits (see Boozy Boba Syrup, page 187), but this is our go-to sweetener, rich with a nice background of depth from the brown sugar. Still, it's got a pretty clean flavor for our classic teas. If you're feeling ambitious, we recommend making syrups out of Asian black sugar, rock sugar, or even Japanese Kuromitsu. That'd make your milk tea next-level next-level.

You can keep this on hand in the fridge for a month.

MAKES ABOUT 2 CUPS

1 cup dark brown sugar, packed

1 cup white sugar

1 cup boiling-hot filtered water

Combine the brown and white sugars in a heatproof bowl. Whisk in the hot water until dissolved.

How Every Boba Tea Contains Thousands of Years of History

8000 BCE: The Roots (Literally) of Boba

You can't have boba without tapioca, which is made from cassava root, which has been a staple food in South America for 10,000 years.

2437 BCE: All the Tea (Is) in China

About 5,000 years ago in China, according to legend, the mythic emperor Shennong was boiling water in a large vat in his back-yard—as you do, when you are the father of Chinese medicine, agriculture, acupuncture, etc. Some leaves from a nearby wild tea tree fell into Shennong's cauldron, and the emperor found them not only delicious but also of clear medicinal value. "Clear" being

the operative word here, because Shennong had a transparent body—as you do, in mythic China. (Seriously, Google him.)

7th Century: Tang Dynasty Tea Tax

The Tang Dynasty (618–907) saw a marked rise in the popular consumption of tea, as evidenced by China's first tea tax. In this era, tea started showing up in Buddhist, Taoist, and Confucian rituals from India to Japan, where, around this time, tea was first ground into a powder and called *matcha*.

13th Century: The West "Discovers" (Eye Roll) Tea

Between 700 and 800 years ago, Portuguese traders first made their way to China and Marco Polo traveled throughout the East, and the West "discovered" tea. It didn't really become a thing until later.

1542: Portuguese Sailors and "Ilha Formosa"

Taiwan, the birthplace of boba, is an island. The Portuguese picked up cassava root, an ancient staple of native peoples in what is now Brazil, and as the Spanish and Portuguese made their presence felt on the Ilha Formosa ("beautiful island"), cassava root worked its way into the diet there.

18th Century: The U.K. Takes to Tea in a Big Way

At the beginning of the 18th century, British men drank coffee, not tea. *Some* British women drank tea, as it was perceived to be a daintier beverage. But the power of the British East India Company rose during the 1700s, and everything changed. As the company established trading monopolies with China, tea showed up in coffeehouses back home in the U.K., sometimes called "China drink" or "tee." Then the empire spread to India, where

the British East India Company annexed land and deployed troops, and that's when Indian black teas, such as Assam and Ceylon, began to appear in coffeehouses.

Since coffee was more in demand throughout Europe than tea was, and since growing the market for tea was a way for the U.K. to expand its empire, the British chose tea as the drink of choice, which it remains to this day.

18th Century: Miffing, Tiffing, and a Spoonful of Sugar

OK, so our eye rolling aside, the truth is: Without British imperialism in Asia, there'd be no boba, because the U.K. is where tea was first mixed with milk and sugar.

Lactose intolerance is rare in Northern Europe, but in parts of Asia, we're genetically

wired for it. We'd never have thought to put milk in tea. So . . . thanks? For your conquest? U.K.? We'll also keep the digs about all of this leading to the Opium Wars to a minimum.

1773: Meanwhile, in the British Colonies of America

It's important to mention that without tea, there probably would be no United States of America (remember how the Boston Tea Party caused the Intolerable Acts, which caused Washington and Jefferson and those dudes to form the First Continental Congress and then, boom, Revolutionary War? Thanks, Westborough Middle School!).

Anyway, because of the British fixation with tea, Americans turned away from it from the start. This part of history is actually important

to us, because it sets up the way boba is perceived as a novelty in America. You couldn't bridge cultures with boba if we'd always drunk tea here!

1940s: A Hong Kong Remix

In the British colony of Hong Kong, people were putting their own spin on the British custom, mixing rich evaporated milk with black tea made from a strong blend, and the popularity of milk tea spread throughout China and Taiwan.

1980s: A Boba Remix

Finally, somebody (see page 16) in Taiwan dropped tapioca balls, a popular topping in snow ice desserts, into a cup of sweetened milk tea, and boba was born. Shelf-stable nondairy powders were key, because they suited the outdoors/nonrefrigerated stall culture of Taiwan's night markets, and they also skirted the whole lactose intolerance issue.

Today: Wait, Yeah, Another Remix— Boba Guys–Style

Oh, yeah, we almost forgot. Now boba's taken root in the U.S., and we're adding stuff like horchata to it, using local milk, and reinventing the form as American boba. So new cultures are mixing in this drink once again.

The Boba Book

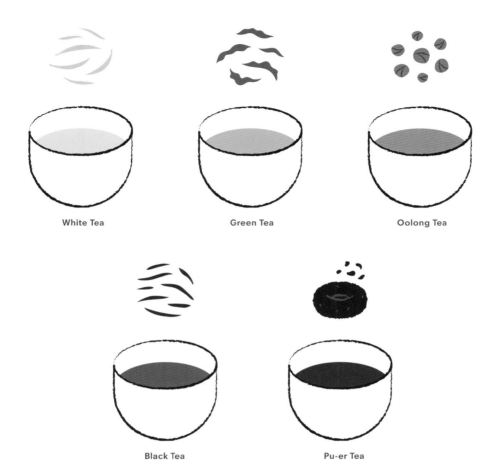

White Tea

Green Tea

Oolong Tea

Black Tea

Pu-er Tea

The Tea Plant

This is *The BOBA Book,* after all, not *The TEA Book,* so just the basics here!

All of what we call "tea" in America comes from a single plant. Its scientific name is *Camellia sinensis*, and it is native to Asia. From this plant, thousands of varieties result. Most distinctions between the different types of tea come from the different ways this plant is processed after it's been picked.

We do know from our sourcing trips to Asia that factors of *terroir* come into play with tea, but generally speaking, that's not something you need to know about to use this book. We hear tea compared to wine a lot. Which is useful to a point. But the comparison is deceptive, because there are so many kinds of grapes used to make wine, but they're all processed in just a handful of ways. The diversity of teas all results from a single plant. It's as if all the wine in the world was made from cabernet grapes.

Generally, all tea is divided into six main categories.

CATEGORIES OF TEA

Types of tea can be categorized in ascending order of how oxidized or manipulated they are. Oxidation is a chemical reaction that happens when tea leaves are exposed to oxygen, which cause changes in appearance (browning) and flavor (deepening).

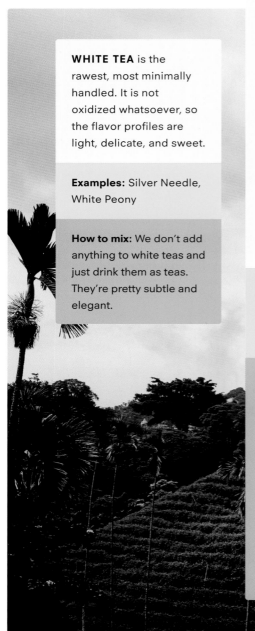

WHITE TEA is the rawest, most minimally handled. It is not oxidized whatsoever, so the flavor profiles are light, delicate, and sweet.

Examples: Silver Needle, White Peony

How to mix: We don't add anything to white teas and just drink them as teas. They're pretty subtle and elegant.

GREEN TEA has all the grassy, tannic, bright-green goodness of a recently picked plant. It's generally not as caffeinated as black tea—although that can change dramatically depending on where it is from and how it is processed—and is known for its medicinal applications and health benefits. Green tea is loaded with antioxidants, for example.

Examples: Matcha, Dragonwell, Gyokuro, Sencha, Jasmine, Hojicha, Biluochun

How to mix: Green teas are great mixers—they have enough flavor to stand out but not to overpower. In a lot of the drinks in this book, we combine green tea with fruit. If you want to mix a green tea with alcohol, we recommend a light beer like Heineken or Michelob, soju, or shochu.

OOLONG TEA is a semi-oxidized tea. It's almost like a cross between a black and a green tea. Its taste can vary widely on a spectrum between those two categories.

Examples: Iron Goddess, Frozen Summit, Wuyi Mountain Teas, Big Red Robe, Milk Oolong

How to mix: Oolong is very versatile, like green tea. You can use stronger alcohol like Baileys, Kahlúa, or rum, and the tea still stands up.

BLACK TEA is the most oxidized of all teas. Oxidation makes the leaves withered and pungent. The flavors in brewed black tea are very pronounced. It tends to be the most tannic of all teas. Black teas are also the most omnipresent teas in the West. (Think Lipton's English Breakfast.)

Examples: Assam, Darjeeling, English Breakfast, Ceylon, Yunnan Black Tea

How to mix: Black tea is tough to work with as a mixer because it has such a strong, tannic flavor. It tends to overpower delicately flavored liquors. You can use very little of it, and mix it with something that will dilute and add texture, like a sturdy, fatty organic milk or milk substitute.

PU-ERH TEA is a fermented tea that tends to have a smoother, sweeter taste than black tea, although when it is brewed, it can have a similar dark liquor. Like wine, pu-erh has the reputation of "the older, the better," although we haven't found this always to be the case. (We find flavor tends to drop after about 75 years.) There are also "raw" and "ripe" pu-erhs. While they are both fermented, raw pu-erhs tend to be cleaner in flavor; ripe ones are fermented wet and can have a mustier flavor.

How to mix: Pu-erh can work with hard alcohol, especially smokier spirits like scotch and mezcal, or anything spicy. A pu-erh old-fashioned by the fire on a misty San Francisco night is just lovely.

HERBAL "TEA" does not come from the *Camellia sinensis*, aka tea plant. Rather—surprise!—it is made from herbs, other plants, or even dried fruits. It is often caffeine-free, and while it can be delicious, it tastes nothing like true tea. Sometimes they're called "tisanes" or "infusions" because "herbal teas" has gotten such a lame reputation, but we like lots of them and use them pretty heavily in this book. (Plus, we're from San Francisco, so we tend to like our herbals a lot.)

The Little Boba Shop that Could

This book is more about drinks and less about us. But we do want to say that there's a shift in the industry and thanks to all of the support from our community, who have been with us since we were just a pop-up, we're a big part of that. If you're a boba fan, you might have noticed that we do things a little differently than most shops. We source our own teas from Asia, we let you choose your own sweetness level in our stores, and we don't make boba from powders and milk substitutes the way many boba shops do. We're all about #nextlevelquality. We're not hating on boba made from powders—we grew up on it!—but we're looking at the future, doing things a little more healthy, getting into plastic straw alternatives, working transparently, and one day we really hope the world can look at our version of boba as a model for the café of the future.

> Hey, guys, this is great and all, but don't you think we should get back to the recipes?

> C'mon, give us our moment to shine!!

> Uh, it's a cookbook, remember?

36

Boba-fy the World!

We want to tell you a quick story about this book.

So we were almost done with this book and we had a minor panic attack. It's not a good time: it's been nearly two years, we're in the home stretch, and the printer is waiting. We were reading the proofs, looking at the amazing pictures, and we still felt something was missing.

The reason is that we don't want to throw away our shot. This page was originally meant to be about straws (TL;DR: get some wide metal boba straws online for these drinks and skip the single-use plastics!), but we decided to use it for something else.

This is about our mandate. In our pitch for this book, we told our publisher that the boba world doesn't get any respect. We want to quote Rodney Dangerfield here, but y'all are probably too young. So as the great poet Drake once said, "We started at the bottom, now we're here."

As more people get to know our style of drinks, we believe boba shops around the country will finally get their due in Western culinary history. This is the first boba book. There will be the first boba show. Then a boba conference. It is only a matter of time. We serve nearly three million unique guests every year—that's more than many of the hottest restaurant groups and cafe concepts in America. And we do that serving drinks that most of the country hasn't heard of before. And our story isn't unique. This is happening in the United Kingdom, Germany, Australia, South Africa. Boba is here to stay.

Our friends and team said our first drafts of this book didn't sound enough like us, the Boba Guys. We said there's no origin story about us in this book because it's not about us. It's about the industry.

Few people know a little boba shop popularized oat milk for the masses. The pousse layering techniques now prevalent in many cafés are a direct result of boba shops. Sweetness adjustments. Yep, boba shops. Milk foam. Boba shops. Toppings like chia seeds or pudding in drinks. Boba shops. Accessible mocktails. Boba shops. Tea cocktails. Boba shops.

When boba shops around the country heard we'd be writing this book, they all had one request: make our industry proud. Well, we woke up just in time. We haven't forgotten who we are.

Now that the engine is revved up . . . let's go!

Tools of the Trade

You don't need anything fancy to make our recipes at home to get the same results we get in our stores. But now that you're a home-style bobarista, here are a few key tools we recommend you have on hand.

The Boba Book

Teas

1. Kettle
2. Fine-mesh strainer, or teapot

Matcha

3. Small whisk
4. Chashaku (small matcha scoop)
5. Bowl

Boba Making

6. Saucepan
7. Small pea ladle (basically a tiny strainer)
8. Wooden spoon

Cocktails

9. Ice cube tray
10. Funnel
11. Citrus juicer
12. Measuring jigger
13. Cocktail shaker
14. Cocktail strainer
15. Bar spoon
16. Muddler

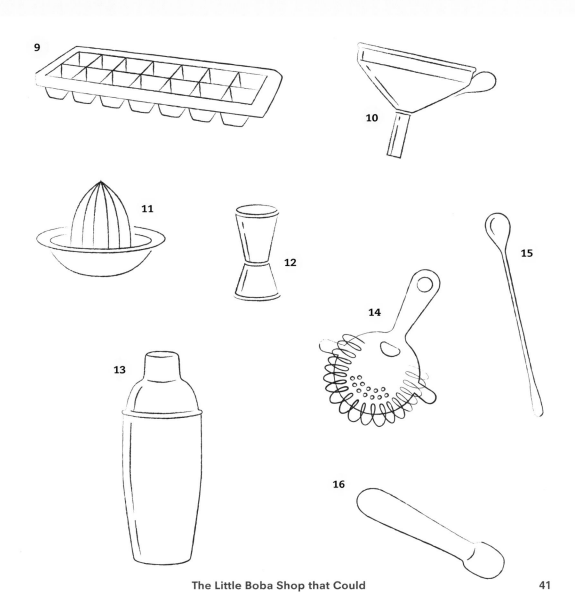

SOUP & SANDWICH

The Childhood Roots of "Bridging Cultures"

ANDREW'S SOUP

Because I grew up as a restaurant brat, most of the rice I ate was leftovers from my family's restaurant, reheated. I loved standing at the stove, heating up my own food. It's what I thought American kids did.

I was the only Asian kid in my class and I felt like the only Asian kid in the entire town of Woodbridge, New Jersey. I didn't know anything about "American food," but I knew that it came already made: TV dinners and cans of soup.

In second grade, I had a friend up the street—Georgie Askins. He had wispy brown hair and a big laugh, and he's one of my closest friends to this day.

I remember going to Georgie's house for dinner and watching his mom pop open

a can of clam chowder. I'd never heard of it, but there was a heavy "plop!" and then a loud hiss as the gelatinous mass hit the hot saucepan. Three minutes later, I had a bowl in front of me. It smelled delicious and was salty and savory, thick with chewy clam meat and soft potato.

The next thing I remember is eyeing that empty can in the sink. What magical thing did I just eat?

I ran to the supermarket.

I brought my can of clam chowder to my grandpa, who was working in the kitchen at my family's restaurant. When I handed him the can, he sighed deeply.

"You eat soup from a can?" he said in Cantonese. "Go up front and have a seat. I'll bring you your soup."

I found a booth to await my special off-menu American dish. The other diners could keep their noodles and dumplings. I was having my Campbell's.

I tucked the cloth napkin into the collar of my shirt like I had seen in TV commercials. I probably looked like a tiny Chinese mob boss: "Leave the duck sauce, take the cannoli."

Finally, one of the waiters brought out my soup. I looked down, puzzled. "What's wrong?" the waiter asked.

"This isn't my soup!" I screamed. I slid out of the booth, and like the tiny petulant Asian mafia boss I was, stormed through the kitchen doors. "Yeh Yeh, this isn't my soup!"

"I made your soup," he said. "It's what was in the can."

My grandpa shrugged me off and turned back to his wok. "Anyways, why do you eat that? The Chinese soup I give you is better," he said, waving me off.

I waddled back to my corner booth and reluctantly ate the clam chowder. It was OK. But it wasn't like at Georgie's house. Nowhere close.

Later that night I knocked on Georgie's door.

"How does your mom make soup?"

Georgie went to the cupboard and pulled out a can.

"It's just clam chowder, Andrew."

"I don't get it. I had it today and it wasn't what your mom makes."

Georgie pointed to the label, the fine print above the large-size "Clam Chowder" script. *New England* Clam Chowder. My can was *Manhattan*. Both clam chowders, but entirely different, from two areas both just a few hours' drive from Woodbridge.

It was like staring at a multiplication table of "American food." Luckily I had a friend who could help show me the ropes. Georgie looked at me endearingly and smiled.

"Take a seat," he said.

He opened a drawer, got out a can opener, and opened up another can of my favorite soup.

BIN'S SANDWICH

Like Andrew, I'm pretty sure I was one of two Asian kids in my town. The other was my brother.

At the tender age of 2, I moved from Taiwan to Wharton, Texas, a town of not even 10,000, 60 miles southwest of Houston. My dad had come earlier and gotten a job at a plastics factory. It was a good job. His dad was a pig farmer who never learned to read. So we all went to America.

There's not much to Wharton. It's a classic roadside small town. There's a little main street of storefronts, a couple of local government buildings, a stoplight, and if you blink, you're already back on that long, flat Texas highway.

Luckily, like Andrew had Georgie, I had a strong, kind influence who taught me how to "America." Her name was Helen Stafford. She was a retired English teacher who volunteered with immigrant families. Ms. Stafford taught me about Christmas, table manners, all these conventions you can struggle to learn if you come to a new country halfway around the world.

But the stuff Ms. Stafford taught me about didn't apply when I was at home with my family. The rule I lived by was "When you're at home, you're Taiwanese; when you're at school, you're American."

One of the Taiwanese things I loved most was pork sung (also called *rousong*, pork floss, meat wool, meat floss—in Vietnamese it's *ruốc*). It's a salty dehydrated meat garnish that we always had in a big plastic jar in the cupboard. It's light and stringy looking, almost like coarse cotton or spun sugar. It's a common topping for Asian food.

At home, we'd throw pork sung over rice, porridge, noodle dishes. It's a salty, meaty seasoning that works with almost anything, especially with *mantou*—fluffy white steamed buns.

When I was a kid, my favorite thing to do with pork sung was to make an American version of a pork sung sandwich.

What you do is you get a slice of Wonder Bread. You pile on pork sung an inch high, then use the palms of your little 7-year-old hands to flatten it with another slice of Wonder Bread. The whole thing becomes a sugary, starchy, salty dough bomb with crunchy meaty flavor crystals embedded in it. It hits all the notes of deliciousness. And it's something you can make by yourself when you're a little kid.

But I'll never forget sitting at the cafeteria at my after-school program in the First Baptist Church when I was in first grade. I broke out the pork sung sandwich I had made for myself, excited to dig in. I didn't have many friends yet, and I wasn't interested in bringing much attention to myself, but the sight of my stringy brown curly meat floss sandwich caused a ruckus.

"Dude, are you eating somebody's HAIR?!?" someone said, and I heard the cruel laughter of kids.

Time slowed down. My cheeks burned with embarrassment. I shrank down in my chair, trying to disappear, but even as I closed my eyes, I could still hear that laughter. And as tight as I tried to hold my eyes shut, I felt like

there was a bright spotlight shining right on my face. In that moment, I was horrified. I had broken the rule. I had tried to bring my Taiwanese-ness outside of our home, and I learned that even something so tasty could get you made fun of.

From then on, I learned to keep my food to myself. I made sure no one saw it.

> Wow, that is pretty heartbreaking.

• • •

BIN: Probably every immigrant kid has a story like that. Being othered just for loving something we consider delicious.

ANDREW: Or a story like mine, where something delicious becomes the bridge to fitting in and assimilating. But you do it in a clumsy kind of way. You need help from the Georgies of the world.

RICHARD: How do you guys reflect on these stories now?

ANDREW: After my first taste of American food, I never looked back: Roy Rogers fried chicken, McDonald's. Hungarian food, sushi, red-sauce Italian places. Thai, Korean, Chinese food that was different from the Cantonese dishes prepared in our restaurants.

RICHARD: 👍 The beauty of American food is that it's not all "American" food.

BIN: I started to play more by the rules. I became a full-on (Asian) American, playing POGs, watching TV, and cheering for the Texas Rangers. I hid my pork sung sandwiches. But I always kept eating them.

RICHARD: You never doubted their deliciousness.

BIN: No way! And these days, I regularly turn my non-Asian friends on to pork floss and everybody agrees: it's just undeniably delicious.

• • •

ANDREW: We think a lot about how food is part of our identities and cultures.

BIN: I think it's because we grew up as third-culture kids.

RICHARD: "Third culture"?

ANDREW: Yeah, it's when you don't feel "fully American" or "fully Asian," but somewhere between.

BIN: You can feel kinda lost, especially as a kid, until you realize you're not, you're just part of a new culture—not one, not the other, but a third.

RICHARD: That's where your obsession with remixing comes from.

ANDREW: Who doesn't love to hear the same song over a hot new beat?

BIN: I think it's also why we're not really fixated on what a lot of people want to talk about with cross-cultural food.

RICHARD: Like, the whole conversation around "appropriation"?

ANDREW: Right. In food, fashion, music—basically anything cultural—we tend to see everything as binaries. People like to ask us, "Can a non-Asian wear a Chinese qipao?" or "Can white people run a boba shop?" But we don't think of everything in terms of is it "cultural appropriation" or "cultural appreciation"? There's another way we think about it. It's how we run our company and train our team . . .

BIN: People shouldn't just show up, cherry pick their favorite things about a culture and start thinking they can rep it, leaving the people who actually grew up with it behind. Culture is inherently contextual. You take parts of it out of context, it doesn't carry the same meaning and significance.

RICHARD: So it's always better to appreciate?

ANDREW: Yes, but what or who defines "appreciation"? The world is always changing, the more cultures come into contact with each other, the closer they can become. It's exhausting to sit there and be constantly judging: "Hey you, ramen burger guy, you're doing it right. You honor the ramen code. But foie gras pho guy, you're doing it wrong!" Who's the culture police?

RICHARD: The first time somebody put boba pearls into sweetened milk tea . . . that was a cultural remix. Was it appreciation? Was it appropriation?

ANDREW: Or before that, the first time somebody put milk into tea.

RICHARD: Tea came from the East, but then it went to the West, where milk and sugar were added, and then it came back to the East, where tapioca pearls got dropped in.

BIN: It's like music producers passing around their samples, adding layers to it each time.

ANDREW: That's why we think it isn't about appreciation versus appreciation. It's about attribution. It's like Genius.com, but for food instead of lyrics. It's citing sources, doing your homework, and giving credit if you put your spin on something. We all have positive and negative experiences with learning each other's cultures and feeling like we belong or don't.

BIN: And we take inspiration from food and drink from other countries all the time, but we always try to keep the history and context in mind and present it respectfully.

RICHARD: There are definitely a lot of influences in your drinks that are not just from Taiwan and China and the U.S.

ANDREW: Absolutely. But we feel as long as we're honest and transparent and *give credit where it's due*, we make culture. That is how we evolve as a society.

RICHARD: What do you mean by give credit?

ANDREW: You know, like when Kanye did "Gold Digger" and sampled Ray Charles, and had Jamie Foxx in the video so you could see the connection.

BIN: Or just putting a footnote on something, like in a book report.

ANDREW: Attribution allows us to make culture in a healthy way. We didn't even get starting on tokenism, objectifying culture, and even Columbusing.

BIN: . . . this isn't a TED Talk.

ANDREW: OK! But I had to flex our Simu Liu #BigAsianEnergy a bit. You know this is the section all the journalists and Reddit are gonna dissect, right?

BIN: I get it, but this *is* a recipe book!

TRADITIONAL DRINKS

Welcome to the world of yin liao, which translates from Mandarin as "drinks." Of course, "traditional" is a tricky word when it comes to boba and yin liao, because things are always changing so fast. In this section, you'll find drinks you might have seen in cafés or in boba shops—drinks that for us are cultural staples. We're trying to honor the classics without too much embellishment in these recipes. We also weight this section heavily toward more entry-level techniques and ingredients; then we level up as we proceed deeper into the book. You'll probably learn a little bit about our childhoods in the stories behind these drinks because we grew up on them. But it's not going to be all stuff you've heard of before. Even for the boba expert, there are bound to be a couple of surprises in this chapter.

ICED MATCHA LATTE

The combination of matcha and milk has been around for a long time—green tea ice cream is at least as old as the 1980s! And matcha lattes started to show up stateside more than 10 years ago. The grassiness and umami of the tea with the creaminess of the milk—and yes, the colors—all make the combination work, even though matcha *traditionally* had nothing to do with milk.

We wanted to take this modern classic combination of matcha and milk, and we wanted to tell a story with it. Which is where the layering technique comes in. You see the tea and the milk in distinct layers, and then you stir them into a cloudy green—it's East meets West, and it's beautiful.

Start with the milk and ice in the glass. Then carefully pour in the tea so it hits the ice and disperses slowly over the top of the milk. If you pour it too fast, the tea will shoot straight through the milk and marbleize the drink.

> Hey guys, why are we opening the "Traditional Drinks" chapter with an Iced Matcha Latte? Isn't that a trendy drink?

> You gotta get the millennials! But seriously, matcha green tea drinks are staples in Asia. To the Japanese and some Chinese, matcha is very sacred.

> Damn, I'm such a gaijin.

> There are tea ceremonies that go back over a millennia. It looks now like a health-and-wellness, chill-with-palm-trees Instagrammer drink, but it's got a storied past that we shouldn't gloss over.

MAKES 1 GLASS

RECOMMENDED TOPPINGS: BOBA, GRASS JELLY, EGG PUDDING

1½ teaspoons premium matcha

3½ tablespoons filtered water, heated to 170°F

1 tablespoon honey

2 to 4 tablespoons toppings of your choice (optional)

1 tablespoon House Syrup (page 27), or to taste

8 ounces (by weight) ice cubes

6 ounces whole milk

Place the matcha in a bowl and add 1 tablespoon of the hot water. Whisk vigorously to make a paste. It should have the consistency of peanut butter with no clumps. Then add the remaining 2½ tablespoons hot water to the matcha and whisk vigorously, until any remaining clumps disappear.

Coat the inside of a glass with the honey (see page 55). Add the toppings, if using, and pour the syrup into the glass. Add the ice and the milk. Then gently pour the matcha over the milk, aiming for the ice cubes to keep the layers cleanly separated. Stir before drinking.

HONG KONG MILK TEA

ANDREW: I grew up on this tea. I'm part Taiwanese, part Cantonese. (So please don't talk to me about Chinese politics!) Cantonese food is totally banging: think char siu bao/pork buns, beef chow fun, and salted fish fried rice. And Hong Kong café culture is *vibrant*, a cross-cultural mix of British, European, and Chinese influences. My grandmother used to make these macaroni soups you see in HK cafés all the time, and she'd serve it with milk tea enriched with evaporated or sweetened condensed milk. The brand that everybody knows is called Longevity. It's got an illustration of an old dude who looks like an Asian Saruman.

When we were first starting Boba Guys, we were considering focusing on Hong Kong teas, but we ended up with Taiwanese boba as our staple. So in an alternate universe, this recipe, instead of the Classic Milk Tea, is the staple drink we would have riffed on.

> For the Cantos out there, you'll notice that all three recommended toppings are traditional Cantonese desserts.

MAKES 1 GLASS

RECOMMENDED TOPPINGS: GRASS JELLY, EGG PUDDING, BLACK STICKY RICE

2 tablespoons sweetened condensed milk

2 to 4 tablespoons toppings of your choice (optional)

5 ounces (by weight) ice cubes

1 tablespoon House Syrup (page 27), or to taste

8 ounces Brewed Boba Guys' Black Tea (page 27)

Coat the inside of a glass with half of the condensed milk (see sidebar opposite). Add the toppings, if using, and the ice. Pour the syrup and the remaining condensed milk over the ice. Pour the tea over the ice. Stir until everything is mixed before drinking.

How to Coat Your Glass

When you're coating the glass, start with a super-thin pour of sweetened condensed milk (or honey, or whatever syrupy matter you are coating your glass with), like streaming in a piece of twine. You want it to hit the inside of the lip of the glass, as close to the top as possible, with the glass at as slight of an angle as possible, so it's almost standing straight up. And then you want to rotate the glass constantly, so rotation after rotation, you're gradually adding the condensed milk. The milk should start floating down the sides of the glass in a sheet. Coating the glass makes the condensed milk mix in a little more easily—the milk is so rich and sticky that it can require some real stirring otherwise—but let's face it, it looks *good* when you get it right.

NOTE:

If you want to make ginger juice, the most effective method is to use a juicer. We do not recommend using a blender or food processor, but if you must, for ½ cup juice, you'll need ¾ pound fresh ginger, blended and squeezed / strained through a few layers of cheesecloth. It's a workout! You can store ginger juice in the fridge for up to 1 week.

TEH TARIK

This is a classic Singaporean/Malaysian drink from which you can (and should) build riffs and variations and remixes. Teh Tarik is more aerated than a Hong Kong milk tea and less bitter than the Taiwanese style. It's pretty much the lightest of all the iconic Asian milk teas. "Pulling" it, meaning pouring it back and forth between two cups, helps to aerate it and gives it even more of a feeling of lightness. And it creates a layer of frothy bubbles on top.

This recipe was created by our friend chef Nora Haron, who helped out a lot with the Southeast Asian recipes in this book. Nora added ginger to the classic presentation of Teh Tarik to spice it up a bit. Get your crazy rich Asian drink on.

> Ah, so, that other definition of "bubble tea"?

> Yes!

> So if you add boba, you can double your bubble trouble?

> Richard.

MAKES 10 TO 12 SERVINGS

RECOMMENDED TOPPINGS: BOBA, COCONUT ALMOND JELLY, JAPANESE COFFEE JELLY

¾ cup black tea leaves

8 cups filtered water, heated to 190°F

½ cup ginger juice (fresh or store-bought; see note opposite)

1 cup sweetened condensed milk, heated

1 cup heavy cream, heated

2 to 4 tablespoons (per cup) toppings of your choice (optional)

Steep the black tea leaves in the hot water for 4 minutes. Then strain the tea into a heatproof pitcher. Add the ginger juice, condensed milk, and heavy cream. Stir to thoroughly mix the contents. Divide the tea into serving cups.

For the "pulled" (or Tarik) effect: For best results, use a handheld milk frother in each cup until you see fine bubbles topping the cup. Or to go old-school, pour some of the tea into a cup; then pour it, from as high a distance as you're comfortable, into another cup. Pour the tea back and forth between the two cups until it is frothy. Add the toppings, if using.

> BTW how do you pronounce "Teh Tarik"?

> TAY TAH-rick.

THAI ICED TEA

Sweet, creamy, and aromatic, Thai iced tea is really good with anything salty, like curries and all the spicy dishes you get at Thai restaurants. It's almost a desert drink, but you get to have it with your meal, so as kids, how could we resist? For most of our drinks at Boba Guys, we leave it to the customers to adjust the sweetness to their taste, but for this, you really want it sweet.

> I still remember getting Thai takeout at my friend Diego's house for the first time in seventh grade, and we ordered Thai iced teas. They came in these giant Styrofoam cups. I fell in love instantly!

> Makes sense! After the Classic Milk Tea, this is usually the gateway Asian milk tea drink for a lot of people because of the prevalence of Thai restaurants.

For us, Thai Iced Tea was also an early example of thinking outside the box with tea. It has mounds of spices in the tea blend. And it's like the OG Instagrammable drink, but way before Instagram. It looks beautiful, with the gentle marbling from the condensed milk in this bright orange tea. It's iconic.

MAKES 1 GLASS

RECOMMENDED TOPPINGS: BOBA, GRASS JELLY

1 tablespoon sweetened condensed milk

2 to 4 tablespoons toppings of your choice (optional)

5 ounces (by weight) ice cubes

1 cup Brewed Thai Tea (recipe follows)

2½ ounces half-and-half

Coat the inside of a glass with the condensed milk (see page 55). Add the toppings, if using, and the ice, and pour the tea over the ice. Add the half-and-half. Stir until everything is mixed before drinking.

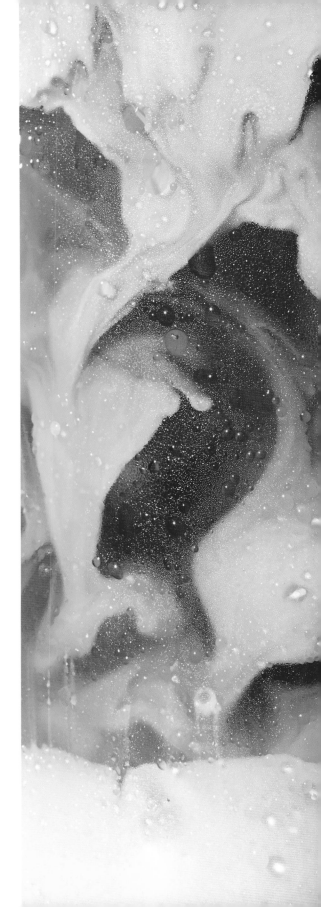

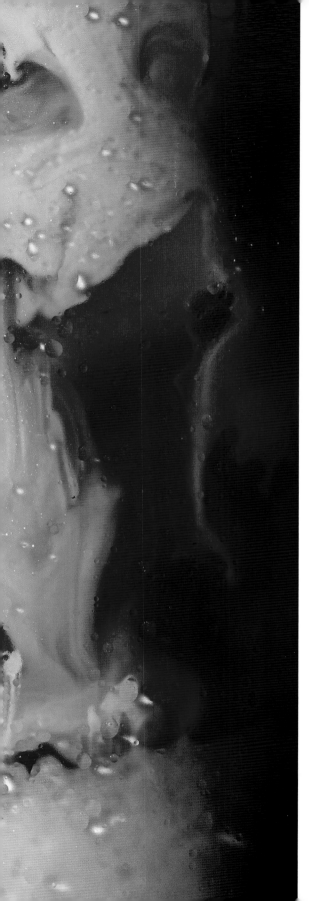

brewed thai tea

MAKES ABOUT 10 CUPS

1 cup white sugar
Thai Tea Blend (recipe follows)
6 cups filtered water, heated to 190°F
5 cups ice cubes

Mix the sugar and Thai tea blend in a heatproof bowl. Add the hot water and steep the tea for 20 minutes.

Fill a pitcher with the ice cubes. Strain the tea over the ice, and set the pitcher aside to allow the ice to fully melt.

Store in an airtight container for up to a week.

thai tea blend

MAKES ENOUGH FOR 10 CUPS

3 whole star anise pods
6 green cardamom pods
1 cinnamon stick, approximately 4 inches long
1 tablespoon vanilla powder
½ cup Ceylon tea leaves

Using a mortar and pestle or a mallet, lightly crush the star anise, cardamom, and cinnamon stick. Mix these thoroughly with the vanilla powder and tea leaves. Store in an airtight container. Keeps for up to a year.

ICED TURMERIC LATTE

Ah . . . the Golden Latte, as some would call it. Turmeric tea and something creamy. We love it. Turmeric is known for its digestive and anti-inflammatory properties. The drink tastes like a blend of mustard, nuts, and ginger. This drink would win a drink decathlon. It's colorful, versatile, healthy, and distinctive to the palate.

So how could such a drink be so divisive? It's not because it's slightly bitter. The cultural conversation around turmeric is a lot like matcha. Both are ingredients with millennia of tradition—Japan for matcha, South Asia for turmeric—so for many, it feels weird to separate this item from its cultural significance. In parts of India, turmeric is used in sacred ceremonies and in regional fashion.

We decided to include a turmeric latte recipe in this book because we hope people who are being introduced to turmeric also take the time to learn about its role in other cultures. We originally wanted to tell you a story about how we once ruined $200 worth of Boba Guys equipment because turmeric stains are notoriously difficult to remove. But that's a story for another day. Today is about building a bridge.

MAKES 1 GLASS

RECOMMENDED TOPPINGS: BOBA

2 tablespoons honey

2 to 4 tablespoons toppings of your choice (optional)

5 ounces (by weight) ice cubes

1 cup almond milk or "coconut beverage" (you can find this at stores like Trader Joe's; it's essentially coconut milk thinned down to a drinkable consistency)

¼ cup Turmeric Tea (recipe follows)

Coat the inside of a glass with honey (see page 55). Add the toppings, if using, and the ice. Pour the almond milk or coconut beverage into the glass. Gently pour the turmeric tea into the glass, aiming for the ice to create a layering effect.

turmeric tea

MAKES 1 CUP

1 cup almond milk

¼ teaspoon ground turmeric

¼ teaspoon ground cinnamon

1 teaspoon grated fresh ginger

½ teaspoon vanilla extract

1 tablespoon honey (optional)

In a small saucepan, cook the almond milk on medium heat until it is almost boiling. Turn the heat to low so the milk is simmering. Whisk in the turmeric, cinnamon, ginger, vanilla extract, and honey, if using. Remove the pan from the heat and allow the mixture to cool. Strain the tea into a cup or mason jar.

You can store the turmeric tea in the fridge for up to 3 days.

chai tea blend

MAKES ENOUGH FOR 6 SERVINGS OF TEA

8 green cardamom pods

4 cinnamon sticks, 3 inches each

3 teaspoons black peppercorns

10 whole cloves

½ cup Ceylon tea leaves

Using a mortar and pestle or a mallet, crush the spices lightly. In a small mixing bowl, combine the spices with the tea leaves. The mixture can be kept in an airtight container for months, until the spices are noticeably diminished in aroma.

CHAI LATTE

We both love Indian food and chai goes hand in hand with that. Shout-out to our favorites, Naan N Curry and Pakwan in San Francisco, where we spent many nights brainstorming ideas for Boba Guys. Chai became our chaser from everything to saag paneer to ghobi gosht (cauliflower and lamb). We know Indian drinks go beyond chai, but this is a staple in our lives.

Our chai blend recipe is trying to get somewhere in the ballpark of an instantly recognizable classic. You kind of empty out your spice cabinet for it.

But of course pretty much every South Asian family has their own recipe for chai. We always respect that and encourage people to try their own special variations—so feel free to play with the ratios and the kinds of spices with this recipe.

MAKES 6 CUPS

RECOMMENDED TOPPINGS: BOBA, GRASS JELLY, EGG PUDDING

6 cups filtered water

4 inches of fresh ginger (about 4 inches total), peeled and thinly sliced

Chai Tea Blend (recipe opposite)

1½ cups half-and-half, heated

6 tablespoons House Syrup (page 27), or to taste

2 to 4 tablespoons (per cup) toppings of your choice (optional)

In a small saucepan, combine the water and ginger and simmer, covered, over medium heat for 15 minutes. (You may need to reduce the heat to keep it at a gentle simmer.)

Bring the water up to 190°F. Remove the pan from the heat and add the chai blend. Steep for 5 minutes.

Strain the tea and divide it evenly among six cups. Mix ¼ cup of half-and-half and 1 tablespoon house syrup into each cup. Add the toppings, if using.

MANGO LASSI

This is another classic Indian drink. The combo of tangy yogurt and sweet mango is exactly what you want when it's hot outside. If you don't feel like eating too much, this will fill you up a bit while cooling you down.

We often get questions on what type of mangoes to use in drinks. The sweeter, the better. We love Carabao from the Philippines or Nam Dok Mai mangoes from Thailand if you can find them. But any sweet, non-stringy mango will work, even frozen ones.

MAKES 1 GLASS

RECOMMENDED TOPPINGS: SAGO, EGG PUDDING

½ cup Mango Puree (recipe follows)

5 ounces (by weight) ice cubes

¼ cup whole milk

¼ cup kefir or drinkable yogurt

½ teaspoon ground cardamom

½ lime, juiced

2 to 4 tablespoons toppings of your choice (optional)

In a blender, combine the mango puree, ice cubes, milk, kefir or yogurt, cardamom, and lime juice. Blend until smooth. Pour the mango lassi into a glass, add the toppings, if using, and serve.

mango puree

MAKES 3 CUPS

1½ cups cold filtered water

1 cup raw cane sugar, preferably turbinado

2 cups diced fresh mango (Buy more mangoes than you think you'll need, because you'll compost the skin and the pit.)

In a blender, combine the water, sugar, and mangoes and blend until smooth. Store in the fridge for up to 7 days.

HORCHATA

Growing up, we always thought of horchata as the Mexican Vitasoy (a sweet soy milk that every Asian drank growing up). Now that we're older, we understand its cultural significance a bit more. When people ask what our first signature drink was, it's our housemade horchata recipe. It's a staple in many Hispanic cultures: traditionally made from rice milk, it's a sweet, spiced drink, a great pairing with spicy savory food. We call Cali our home, so horchata is particularly near and dear to our hearts as you'll find versions of it in most taquerias and local supermarkets.

Our original horchata recipe came in a lot of local inspiration, including our favorites, La Balompié and Taqueria Cancun in the Mission District in San Francisco. We want to thank everyone in the neighborhood for teaching two Asian guys something so near and dear to your hearts.

We love the combination of whole and rice milks here, but you can also try switching out the whole milk for some really good, thick almond milk to get a nuttier flavor, closer to the Spanish or Salvadorian styles of horchata.

You can enjoy this on its own without mixing it into one of our drinks.

MAKES ABOUT 8 GLASSES

RECOMMENDED TOPPINGS: JAPANESE COFFEE JELLY, EGG PUDDING, BOBA

6 tablespoons white sugar

2½ teaspoons vanilla powder

½ teaspoon ground cinnamon

1 cup whole milk

6½ cups rice milk

2 to 4 tablespoons (per glass) toppings of your choice (optional)

In a pitcher, combine the sugar, vanilla powder, and cinnamon. Pour the whole milk into the pitcher and stir. Add the rice milk and mix thoroughly. Serve, with the toppings, if desired.

You can store this in the fridge for up to 1 week.

ICED CHAMPURRADO

When we started out as a pop-up in the Mission District of San Francisco, we'd be carrying our equipment out to our car at the end of those long nights and we would smell the sweet, spicy aroma of champurrado filling the cool night air. It's a hot Mexican corn-thickened chocolate-and-spice milk drink, and it'd be impossible to resist. It's always cold in San Francisco.

> As Mark Twain supposedly said, "The coldest winter I ever spent was a summer in San Francisco."

> Yes, Professor.

So champurrado always hits the spot in the most comforting, warming way. You can have boba drinks hot or cold, so pick whatever is to your liking, but we love this one cold.

MAKES 1 GLASS

RECOMMENDED TOPPINGS: BOBA, EGG PUDDING

2 to 4 tablespoons toppings of your choice (optional)

5 ounces (by weight) ice cubes

1 cup Champurrado (recipe follows), cool or room temperature

Put the toppings, if using, in a glass, and add the ice. Pour in the champurrado.

champurrado

MAKES 6 SERVINGS

½ cup masa harina or corn flour (not cornstarch)

3 cups filtered water

1 teaspoon ground cinnamon

2 whole star anise pods

½ teaspoon salt

2 ounces (¼ cup packed) dark brown sugar or piloncillo

4 ounces dark/bittersweet chocolate

¼ teaspoon cayenne pepper

3 cups whole milk

In a medium-size saucepan, slowly whisk the masa harina or corn flour into the water. Add the cinnamon, star anise, and salt. Cook over medium heat, whisking, until the mixture thickens and is almost simmering.

Turn the heat down to low and add the brown sugar, chocolate, and cayenne pepper. Mix until the sugar and chocolate are completely dissolved.

Slowly whisk in the milk until thoroughly mixed. Remove from the heat and, for best texture, strain the champurrado through a fine-mesh sieve into a container. Let it cool.

You can store the champurrado in an airtight container in the fridge for up to 2 weeks.

POG

POG! So classic. So its own thing. This is just pretty much the Hawai'ian standard you know and love. (Or if you don't, you're about to.) The classic combination of passion fruit plus orange plus guava was created in the 1970s at Haleakala Creamery in Maui. We don't mess with it too much. You get that nice tartness and sweetness from the fruit in this combination, but we use a bit more pulp than most might because, you know, chewing your drink. Use fresh-squeezed juice if possible.

And a little fun history: The caps to the bottles that POG is traditionally served in became collectors' items and then that morphed into a game. Milk cap games had been played in Hawai'i, according to some reports, since as early as the 1920s. The game of POG we grew up with, which was big in the '90s, was an update of that game. You'd stack a bunch of POG caps (they weren't even bottle caps anymore, but that's what they were called), then you'd try to upset the stack with a "slammer." Whichever caps landed faceup, you got to keep. Then you'd keep your winnings until the next game. While developing this recipe we had fun reminiscing about our old POG "slammers," which you could buy in baseball card shops back in the day: Beavis and Butt-Head, yin and yang, skull and crossbones . . . kids of the '90s, you know what we're talking about!

MAKES 6 SERVINGS

RECOMMENDED TOPPINGS: GRASS JELLY, CENDOL, TAPIOCA CHIA SEED PUDDING

2 cups passion fruit pulp (or store-bought puree)

1 cup orange juice

1 cup guava juice

½ cup pineapple juice

¼ cup honey

Ice cubes, as desired

2 to 4 tablespoons (per glass) toppings of your choice (optional)

In a blender, process the passion fruit pulp on medium-low speed to break up the seeds and puree the pulp. Strain out the seeds with a fine-mesh strainer and return the strained puree to the blender. (If you're using bottled puree, no need to strain. Just pour it into the blender.) Add the orange, guava, and pineapple juices and the honey. Blend on low speed. Then either blend in ice cubes to make a slushie, or serve the juice over ice. Add the toppings, if desired.

You can store the blended juice in the fridge for up to a week.

VIETNAMESE ICED COFFEE

Vietnam is known for its sweet, strong coffee drinks. You can't write a book about Asian drinks without mentioning the iconic Vietnamese iced coffee. We do it with a homemade macadamia nut condensed milk because we like the idea that Hawai'i and Southeast Asia are shaking hands in this cup, but you can go old-school and just use the standard sweetened condensed milk instead. For the full effect, you'll want to get a Vietnamese coffee filter, which is a simple single-serving dripper you set on top of your glass. They're readily available in Asian markets and online. For the coffee, you can use your favorite dark-roast coffee, or do like they do in New Orleans and use a coffee-chicory blend, or add some ground chicory to the dark roast.

MAKES 1 GLASS

RECOMMENDED TOPPINGS: JAPANESE COFFEE JELLY, EGG PUDDING, BLACK STICKY RICE

1½ tablespoons coarsely ground dark roast coffee beans

½ teaspoon ground chicory (optional)

2 to 4 tablespoons toppings of your choice (optional)

2 tablespoons Macadamia Nut Condensed Milk (recipe follows) or sweetened condensed milk, or to taste

8 ounces (by weight) ice cubes

5 ounces (½ cup + 2 tablespoons) filtered water, heated to 200°F

Unscrew the filter plate in a Vietnamese coffee filter and add the ground coffee and chicory, if using, to it. Screw the filter plate back on, but not too tight. (The tighter you set it, the slower the drip and the stronger the coffee.) Set the filter aside.

Put the toppings, if using, in a glass, and add the condensed milk and the ice. Place the coffee filter over the top of the glass and fill the filter with the hot water. Allow the coffee to slowly drip into the glass; this will take 4 to 5 minutes. If necessary, continue adding hot water as the coffee drips out. Once the dripping has stopped, stir the drink to combine.

macadamia nut condensed milk

Not even King Kamehameha could have dreamed of this. Of course, back then, macadamia nuts weren't even harvested from the trees in Hawai'i. They were considered to be too beautiful to be a crop. But their creamy flavor is transcendent, and we love using them to make a rich condensed milk alternative. Note that this isn't a dairy-free version—we just love how the nuts infuse the milk with their flavor.

MAKES 1½ CUPS, ENOUGH FOR ABOUT 10 SERVINGS

1 cup macadamia nuts
2 cups whole milk
¾ cup cane sugar
¼ teaspoon salt
2 teaspoons vanilla extract

Using a food processor, grind the macadamia nuts until they form a paste. In a medium saucepan, cook the nut paste on medium-high heat, stirring, for 5 minutes, or until it is very fragrant but not burning. Transfer the nut paste to a bowl.

In the same saucepan, combine the milk and the sugar. Cook over low heat until the sugar has dissolved, then raise the heat to medium-low. Cook, whisking often, until the milk has reduced by half, about 30 minutes. Add the nut paste, salt, and vanilla extract. Whisk together until everything is thoroughly combined. Remove from the heat. Allow to cool.

Store the mixture in a mason jar or other airtight container in the fridge for up to 1 week.

VIETNAMESE EGG SODA

The combination of fizzy soda and creamy richness is totally delicious. This Vietnamese drink takes that idea and goes hard on it, adding egg yolk. This drink is on the sweeter side, so it's a real treat, somewhere between a drink and a dessert.

MAKES 1 GLASS

RECOMMENDED TOPPINGS: BOBA, JAPANESE COFFEE JELLY

1 large egg yolk

3 tablespoons sweetened condensed milk

Leaves from 1 sprig fresh mint

2 to 4 tablespoons toppings of your choice (optional)

5 ounces (by weight) ice cubes

8 ounces seltzer or club soda

In a small mixing bowl, whisk together the egg yolk and condensed milk.

In a glass, use a muddler or a spoon to smash the mint leaves. Pour the egg yolk mixture into the glass. Add the toppings, if using, the ice, and the seltzer or club soda. Mix vigorously.

VIETNAMESE EGG COFFEE

This is a bit of a riff on both the Vietnamese Iced Coffee (page 72) and the Vietnamese Egg Soda (page 74). We take the rich element of the soda—the combination of condensed milk and egg yolk—and refashion it as a topping for a hot Vietnamese coffee. Using a dark roast coffee is very important here. Lighter roasts are cool these days, highlighting the beans' fruitiness and acidity, but let's face it, our parents never go in for lighter roasts. Dark roast is more old-school, which is the vibe we like for this drink, and a dark roast stands up to the sweetness and richness of the egg cream.

MAKES 2 GLASSES

RECOMMENDED TOPPINGS: BOBA, EGG PUDDING, JAPANESE COFFEE JELLY

3 tablespoons coarsely ground dark-roast coffee beans

1¼ cups filtered water, heated to 200°F

Whipped Egg Cream (recipe follows)

1 to 2 tablespoons (per glass) toppings of your choice (optional)

Unscrew the filter plate of two Vietnamese coffee filters, and divide the coffee grounds between them. Screw the filter plates back on, but not too tight. Place a coffee filter over the top of each glass. Fill the filters with the hot water. If necessary, continue adding hot water as the coffee drips out. Allow the coffee to slowly drip into the glasses, which will take 4 to 5 minutes.

Meanwhile, whisk together the whipped egg cream (see below).

Once the coffee is done dripping, divide the whipped egg cream between the glasses. Add the toppings, if using. Mix together before drinking.

---

whipped egg cream

MAKES ENOUGH FOR 2 GLASSES

2 large egg yolks
2 teaspoons sugar
6 tablespoons sweetened condensed milk

In a small mixing bowl, whisk together the egg yolks, sugar, and condensed milk. Using an electric whisk, whisk for 5 minutes or until the mixture becomes foamy.

COCONUT PANDAN DRINK

Pandan—everywhere in Asia, hardly anywhere in America. It's a South Asian plant that imparts a sweet, floral, vanilla-like quality to savory and sweet dishes alike. Pandan is the Drake of Asian flavoring. Put it in anything. It'll be a hit.

I sure hope this joke ages well.

Culture doesn't always age well.

We're gonna have to come back to that.

Pandan jelly is common in the Philippines, Vietnam, and Thailand. So we like to use it in this drink as a nod to those traditions. Sago is basically the Southeast Asian version of tapioca pudding; the pearls are way smaller and softer than boba, but we're equal-opportunity tapioca lovers.

With the addition of tender sago, the firm-melting texture of the pandan-agar jelly, and the coconut milk, this is a complex, rich drink you can chew—sure to be a showstopper if you want to impress friends who love delicious new flavors.

MAKES 1 GLASS

RECOMMENDED (ADDITIONAL) TOPPINGS: CENDOL, TAPIOCA CHIA SEED PUDDING, CHÈ BA MÀU JELLY

1 tablespoon sweetened condensed milk

2 tablespoons Sago (page 198)

1 tablespoon diced Pandan Jelly (recipe follows)

1 to 2 tablespoons additional toppings of your choice (optional)

5 ounces (by weight) ice cubes

1 cup coconut beverage (you can find this at stores like Trader Joe's; it's essentially coconut milk thinned down to a drinkable consistency)

½ teaspoon pandan extract

Coat a glass with the condensed milk (see page 55). Add the sago topping and pandan jelly to the glass. Add any additional toppings, if using, and the ice. Pour the coconut beverage over the ice. Add the pandan extract. With a spoon, mix everything together thoroughly before drinking.

pandan jelly

1½ cups filtered water

2 tablespoons white sugar

1 tablespoon pandan extract

2½ tablespoons agar powder

In a medium saucepan, bring the water to a boil over medium-high heat. Add the sugar and the pandan extract. Bring the water back to a boil and whisk in the agar powder. Once the powder is fully dissolved, pour the liquid into a heatproof storage container, preferably one with a wide surface to make later cutting easier. Allow the liquid to cool, then store it in the fridge overnight or until firm.

Dice the jelly into small cubes. Store it in the fridge for up to 1 week.

AIR MATA KUCING

This is another Malaysian dish. It's so tropically muggy out there, you can imagine how crushable any super-fruity drink would be in such a hot and humid setting. If you hear "tropical fruit" and automatically think "pineapple and passion fruit," well, we don't blame you. But this is different.

One of the keys to this drink is the longan (pronounced lung-AHN in Cantonese and literally means "dragon's eye"), which looks and tastes similar to a lychee. When longan is dried, its flavor is almost candied. And we knew we wanted to use winter melon in this book somewhere, because it's such an iconic ingredient in our culture's cooking. It's not super sweet, but it cooks up into a smooth, clear, creamy but light texture.

You'll be drinking this all summer long; it's like a fruit substitute for sweet tea.

> As the oldest son in my family, I always had my fruit peeled for me. Longans can be tough to peel, so this drink always has a special place in my heart.

> LOL, must be nice!

> That's a very Asian thing. I was the "golden child."

> I was the oldest son, too. Nobody peeled anything for me.

MAKES 6 TO 8 SERVINGS

RECOMMENDED TOPPINGS: BOBA

6 cups filtered water

1 cup dried monk fruit, diced and loosely packed

¼ cup dried longan

2 cups julienned fresh winter melon

¾ cup rock sugar

2 to 4 tablespoons (per glass) toppings of your choice (optional)

In a medium pot over medium-high heat, bring the water to a boil. While waiting for the water to boil, crush the monk fruit. When the water boils, add the crushed monk fruit and dried longan. Allow the water to come back up to a boil. Add the winter melon and the rock sugar. Bring the contents back up to a boil and then reduce the heat to a simmer. Simmer, partially covered, for 15 to 20 minutes, until the flavors meld. Remove the pot from the heat and allow the contents to rest for 1 hour.

Serve hot or over ice. Add the boba, if desired, before serving. This will keep in an airtight container in the fridge for up to 3 days.

ICED LEMONGRASS CHRYSANTHEMUM TEA

Chrysanthemum tea, the kind that came in a yellow juice box with a flower on the front, is one of the top Chinatown staples of our childhood. It tastes like flowers, but in a totally delicious, even-kids-will-like-it way. You can still find it in many Asian markets. The funny thing is, this "tea drink," as it says on the box, is not even tea! But of course, as you know by now, the fact that it's not tea won't stop us!

Chrysanthemum, like many "herbal" or non-tea teas, can help reduce inflammation and mitigate anxiety, and it is also a source of vitamins A and C. But what's important to us is that this drink is honoring that little yellow juice box. For our twist, we mix in a little lemongrass for that unmistakably citrusy herbal flavor that you find in Thai cuisine.

We use rock sugar because it's a typically Asian thing and it has a rounder, more brown-sugar-like taste. Look for it in Asian markets or online; it will have a yellow or brownish tint and often comes in irregular "rocks," or sometimes in flat cakes.

MAKES 1 GLASS

No toppings?

We're kind of purist on this one. You want to really taste everything that's in the drink in perfect uninterrupted harmony.

RECOMMENDED TOPPINGS: NONE

5 ounces (by weight) ice cubes

1 cup Brewed Lemongrass Chrysanthemum Tea (recipe follows), chilled

2 tablespoons Rock Sugar Syrup (recipe follows)

Put the ice in a glass. Pour the tea over the ice, add the syrup, and stir to mix everything together before drinking.

brewed lemongrass chrysanthemum tea

MAKES 1 CUP TEA

2 tablespoons Lemongrass Chrysanthemum Blend (recipe follows)

5 ounces (½ cup + 2 tablespoons) filtered water, heated to 180°F

4 ounces (by weight) ice cubes

In a heatproof bowl, steep the chrysanthemum blend in the hot water for 4 minutes.

Put the ice cubes in a glass, strain the tea over the ice, and allow the ice to fully melt.

lemongrass chrysanthemum blend

MAKES 1 CUP

⅔ cup dried chrysanthemum flowers

⅓ cup dried lemongrass

Combine the chrysanthemum and lemongrass in a mixing bowl; stir well to fully mix. Store in an airtight container.

rock sugar syrup

MAKES ABOUT 1 CUP

½ cup filtered water
1 cup rock sugar pieces

In a small saucepan, bring the water to a boil over high heat. When the water begins boiling, add the rock sugar and cook, stirring occasionally, until it fully dissolves. Let the syrup cool. It can be kept in the fridge for 2 weeks.

Use leftovers as a sweetener in place of honey, sugar, etc.

HALO HALO

This is one of our favorite desserts of all time. *Halo halo* is, like, *the* iconic Filipino dessert. It usually consists of some combination of pudding, rice, other starches, and coconut meat, topped with condensed milk, and a scoop of bright purple ube ice cream. Andrew grew up in South San Francisco and Daly City, which are heavily Filipino areas, so there were lots of trips after school for this hefty, beautiful sweet dish. And when Bin moved to San Francisco, he got into halo halo, too. (Mitchell's Ice Cream, the S.F. institution, has a great ube ice cream, by the way!) And for us, we top it all off with some Rice Krispies.

> Bridging cultures!

> Yes! We wanted to bring American cereal into a Filipino dessert.

> I just like how you can see and taste each part of the recipe.

> Did we ever tell you we almost made our mission statement "blending cultures"? But we decided against it for that same reason. "Bridging cultures" is about connecting each unique ingredient, not mixing it all together.

> That's deep . . . like Halo Halo.

MAKES 1 GLASS

RECOMMENDED TOPPINGS: NONE

¼ cup Ube Jam (page 137)

2 tablespoons Egg Pudding (page 201)

2 tablespoons Tapioca Balls, aka Boba (page 186)

2 tablespoons Grass Jelly (page 191)

5 ounces (by weight) shaved or finely crushed ice

¾ cup coconut beverage (you can find this at stores like Trader Joe's; it's essentially coconut milk thinned down to a drinkable consistency)

2 tablespoons chopped jackfruit (fresh or frozen)

1 tablespoon Rice Krispies

Coat the inside of a large glass with the ube jam (see page 137). Spoon the egg pudding, boba, and grass jelly into the glass. Add the shaved ice. Pour the coconut beverage over the ice. Top the glass with the jackfruit and Rice Krispies. Serve with a long spoon, and mix while you eat and drink it.

RED BEAN LATTE

I still think about the red bean topping on that massive shaved ice I had in that stall in Taichung.

In the U.S. we generally think of beans as savory and people look at you weird if you tell them about sweet beans in Asian desserts. (Except you eat Boston baked beans with molasses? What's up with that?) But sweetened cooked red beans are perfect for a smoothie or dessert topping. The red beans have a relatively soft skin and break down as they cook, making a perfect puree. This drink is essentially a red bean milkshake, taking the soft, nutty flavor of the bean and blending it with coconut milk. It's more filling than a lot of our drinks, a great protein-rich snack. And it's super easy to make.

You can probably find canned sweetened red beans in many markets, like Whole Foods, these days. If you're shopping for them dried, look for the smaller beans, usually adzuki beans—not, like, New Orleans red beans. Once you find a source for them, you'll probably become addicted to this drink as a morning or afternoon treat.

MAKES 1 GLASS

RECOMMENDED TOPPINGS: BLACK STICKY RICE, BOBA

2 to 4 tablespoons toppings of your choice (optional)

¼ cup Red Bean Puree (recipe follows)

5 ounces (by weight) ice cubes

1 cup rice milk

Put the toppings, if using, in a glass. Then add the red bean puree and the ice. Gently pour the rice milk over the ice to evenly layer the drink. Mix the drink before serving.

red bean puree

MAKES ABOUT 3 CUPS

1 can (15 ounces) sweetened red beans
1 cup unsweetened coconut milk
½ cup white sugar

In a blender, combine the red beans, coconut milk, and sugar. Blend until smooth. Store in the fridge for up to 1 week.

The Boba Book

Global Café Speak

You might notice that throughout this book, what you might call a "shake" or a "smoothie" we sometimes call a "latte." It's a nod to the global café culture we see ourselves as a part of—in many of the Asian cafés we're inspired by, that term has been embraced to cover all kinds of non-coffee drinks. The word "latte" is "milk" in Italian . . . so any drink that's mostly made out of a milk is now considered a latte. And it elevates the ingredients a bit. Like, a red bean or sweet potato "shake" doesn't sound as respectable as a "latte" to us. And that's what you see at boba shops nowadays, so just go with it!

AVOCADO SMOOTHIE

We love avocado smoothies! It may seem like more millennial bait, but avocado smoothies have been a part of Vietnamese, Indonesian, and Filipino cuisine for a long time. The avocado acts like an ice cream here. It provides all the fat and heft you'd get in an ice cream smoothie—er, a shake.

There are tons of ways to riff on this: add blueberries, chocolate, banana—basically any type of fruit flavor or sweetness. Feel free to try those variations on your own.

MAKES 3 GLASSES

RECOMMENDED TOPPINGS: BOBA

2 ripe avocados

2 limes, juiced

1 cup whole milk

½ cup sweetened condensed milk

4 ounces (by weight) ice cubes

2 to 4 tablespoons (per glass) toppings of your choice (optional)

Cut the avocados in half, remove the pits, and scoop the flesh into a blender. Add the lime juice, whole milk, condensed milk, and ice cubes. Blend until smooth.

Add the toppings, if using, to three glasses. Pour the smoothie into the glasses, and serve.

ICED SWEET POTATO LATTE

OK, we know. Who wants to drink a potato? For whatever reason, this really works! When we tried this sweet-potato-and-milk drink in a popular all-day market in Taichung, we were convinced of its deliciousness. It's hefty and a bit savory, but with both natural sweetness from the potato and two kinds of sugar. Combine that with the creaminess, and you can take one of these down easily without thinking of the word "tuber."

But then we had an argument over whether we should offer this in our stores. Who would buy a blended potato? It was a huge fight among all of us at Boba Guys in the early days. To this day, we've never put it on our menu, but we all always order one when we see it on someone else's menu. So here was our compromise: We promised ourselves we'd put it in the book!

MAKES 1 GLASS

RECOMMENDED TOPPINGS: BOBA

¼ cup Roasted Sweet Potato Puree (recipe follows)

2 to 4 tablespoons toppings of your choice (optional)

5 ounces (by weight) ice cubes

1 cup whole milk

In a glass, place the puree and toppings, if using, at the bottom. Add the ice and the milk. Mix before serving.

roasted sweet potato puree

MAKES 1 CUP

6 ounces (1 small) sweet potato
½ cup white sugar
½ cup dark brown sugar
½ cup filtered water

Preheat the oven to 400°F.

Use a paring knife to score the potato, making 1- to 2-inch-long slashes, just deep enough to pierce the skin, all over. Bake the sweet potato for 30 minutes or until a paring knife can poke all the way through without resistance. Allow the sweet potato to cool, then peel it.

In a blender, combine the sweet potato, white and brown sugars, and water. Blend until smooth. If you want, you can put the puree through a fine-mesh strainer for a smoother texture. Store it in the fridge for up to 7 days.

BLACK SESAME LATTE

You guys are totally NUTS!

You're fired.

Nutty, nutty, nutty. This drink is so nutty it's almost meaty, which doesn't really make sense until you drink it. We don't use dairy with this—always good-quality thick almond milk. You want that interplay of sesame and almond.

MAKES 1 DRINK

RECOMMENDED TOPPINGS: BOBA, GRASS JELLY, EGG PUDDING

2 to 4 tablespoons toppings of your choice (optional)

5 ounces (by weight) ice cubes

1 cup unsweetened, unflavored almond milk (use the rich, thick stuff, like Califia or Elmhurst Milked Almonds, and if you can't find those, Almond Breeze can be found at most grocery stores)

¼ cup Black Sesame Puree (recipe follows)

In a glass, add the toppings, if using, and the ice. Pour the almond milk over the ice. Gently spoon the black sesame puree over the ice to help with the layering effect. Mix before drinking.

NOTE:

Ginger syrup can be store-bought, or you can simply simmer a few slices of fresh ginger in a mixture of 1 cup water and 1 cup granulated sugar. The syrup can be stored in the fridge for a few weeks.

black sesame puree

MAKES 3 CUPS (12 SERVINGS)

2 cups roasted black
sesame seeds

1 tablespoon ginger syrup
(see note opposite)

1 cup honey

1 cup whole milk

In a blender, combine the
sesame seeds, ginger syrup,
honey, and milk. Blend
on medium speed until
smooth. The consistency
should be that of a loose
paste. Store the puree in
the refrigerator for up to
3 days.

ROASTED BANANA MILK

You already have all these ingredients in your house, so there's no excuse not to make this today. Actually, you should make it in a few days, because you want your bananas to be super-ripe, like fully brown—the same way you want them for banana pudding, banana bread, or banana cream pie. There isn't anything you need to worry about for presentation for this one, because everything just gets blended up together. This drink is fantastic in the late afternoon. When those pre-dinner hunger pangs hit, this will tide you over and give your mood a little lift, too.

MAKES 1 GLASS

RECOMMENDED TOPPINGS: COCONUT CHIA PUDDING, COCONUT ALMOND JELLY, JAPANESE COFFEE JELLY

¼ cup Banana Jam (recipe follows)

5 ounces (by weight) ice cubes

1 cup whole milk

2 to 4 tablespoons toppings of your choice (optional)

In a blender, combine the jam, ice, and milk and blend on medium speed until smooth.

Add toppings to a glass, if using, and pour the drink into the glass.

banana jam

MAKES 2 CUPS

4 ripe (dark brown) bananas
1 cup packed light brown sugar
3 tablespoons fresh lemon juice
¼ teaspoon ground cinnamon
¼ to ½ teaspoon kosher salt (to taste)

Preheat the oven to 400°F.

Peel the bananas and slice them in half lengthwise. Cut those halves into ½-inch-thick pieces and place them in a mixing bowl. Add the brown sugar, lemon juice, and cinnamon, and toss thoroughly to coat the banana pieces. Line a baking sheet with parchment paper, and spread the bananas out in an even layer on the parchment.

Roast the bananas until they are caramelized, about 15 minutes. Take them out of the oven and set them aside to cool. Once the bananas are cool, place them in a food processor and process until smooth. Add salt to taste.

The banana jam will keep in the fridge for 1 week.

black tea syrup

MAKES ABOUT 1¼ CUPS

½ cup black tea leaves
1 cup filtered water, heated to 200°F
1 cup turbinado sugar

Steep the black tea in the hot water for 12 minutes.

Put the sugar in a container such as a mason jar. Strain the tea into the jar and mix until the sugar is fully dissolved. Allow to cool.

COFFEE TEA "PLOVER"

Our friends at Andytown Coffee in San Francisco, Michael McCrory and Lauren Crabbe, make a signature drink called a "Snowy Plover." It's a coffee-based drink that tastes like a mocktail of sparkling water, cola syrup, and whipping cream. This drink honors Michael's Irish roots as it's their riff on Irish coffee.

We've been working with them for years, so as an homage, we made our own version, using an intense tea-infused syrup as the sweetener, a healthy splash of cold brew coffee, and salted buttercream topping because . . . fancy. It's perfect on a misty, overcast day, which in San Francisco, is pretty much any day.

MAKES 1 GLASS

RECOMMENDED TOPPINGS: BOBA, COCONUT ALMOND JELLY

¼ cup Black Tea Syrup (recipe opposite)

2 to 4 tablespoons toppings of your choice (optional)

5 ounces (by weight) ice cubes

1 cup sparkling water

¼ cup Cold Brew Coffee (see page 151)

2 tablespoons Salted Buttercream Topping (page 113)

Pour the black tea syrup into a glass, and add the toppings, if using, and the ice. Slowly pour in the sparkling water. Gently pour the cold brew over the ice, making sure to aim for the ice cubes to help with the layering effect. Top with the buttercream. Mix all together before drinking.

UME (JAPANESE GREEN PLUM) SODA

This is a deceptively simple drink. Just two ingredients. Ume—the Japanese plum—in syrup form, mixed with soda and served on ice. But you have to learn some new techniques you prob-

> And it involves one of my favorite processes: fermentation!

ably haven't used before to pull it off, and chances are, you've never had these flavors in a drink.

To make this syrup, you layer the plums with sugar and leave them on the counter. The fermentation will break down the fruit and add complex flavor. You can also use this technique for almost any fruit, but it works particularly well with ume plums, which are commonly preserved in Japan.

It might be tricky for you to find fresh ume. It's a summertime special, usually available just from April through June, even in California, where we live and where most of our stores are. When the season is on, you can find ume in many Asian stores and in well-stocked produce markets in big cities. You can always buy the ume when it's in season and then freeze it. Actually, it will start breaking down when you freeze and defrost it, and honestly, we feel like this brings the flavor out even more.

But also, if it isn't ume season and you want to get some delicious practice in on this recipe, you can try the rock-sugar-preserving technique with another fruit, like plums!

MAKES 1 GLASS

RECOMMENDED TOPPINGS: FRESCA KONJAC JELLY

1 fermented ume, from Fermented Ume (Green Plum) Syrup, (page 100)

2 to 4 tablespoons toppings of your choice (optional)

5 ounces (by weight) crushed ice

2 tablespoons Fermented Ume (Green Plum) Syrup (recipe follows)

1 cup sparkling water

Place the fermented ume in a glass and add the toppings, if using. Add the crushed ice. Drizzle the syrup over the ice and add the sparkling water. Mix before drinking.

fermented ume (green plum) syrup

MAKES ABOUT 1½ CUPS

9 ounces (about 6) ume plums
(see note)

1 cup + 2 tablespoons rock sugar

In a 1-quart mason jar, cover the bottom with as many ume as will fit comfortably. Add a layer of sugar on top of the ume. Repeat this process until all the ume and sugar are used up. Store the jar in a cool, dark, dry place. Shake the jar every day. (When the ume liquefies, you can just shake it every couple of days.) The contents of the jar should break down and the scent should deepen. You also might notice bubbles forming—this is normal. The plums should be totally soft after about 7 days. When they are, strain the plums, reserving the syrup (you can discard the pits). Taste your syrup. If you like, you can keep fermenting the syrup and plums in a cool, dark, dry area for up to another 8 weeks. Taste the syrup every day to make sure you like where the flavor is headed.

When the syrup tastes to your liking, separate it from the plums and move them to separate airtight containers. Store the syrup and plums in the fridge for up to 3 months. Use the plums as a garnish, and the syrup in drinks.

We should probably mention that fermentation is a pretty dynamic process, and it depends a lot on weather, temperature in your home, and variables we can't predict.

True. The main thing is to trust your instincts when fermenting and play around with time and other variables and taste as you go.

And if you want to go deeper with fermentation, check out Sandor Katz's *The Art of Fermentation*!

And check out Richard's podcast, too.

The logo is me as a pickle, with a mustache.

NOTE:

If fresh ume aren't available, use frozen or replace with any plum.

Humans of Boba Guys

SPECIALTY DRINKS

These drinks are remixes or reinventions of things we've seen around the world, or are inspired by signature drinks from other cafés we like. (We always like to give credit where it's due!) We've served about half of these drinks in Boba Guys stores. The other half are new drinks we developed specifically for this book and hope to put on our menus soon. Some of these feature slightly more involved techniques and methods, and some have harder-to-find ingredients, but we promise they're worth it. And there are a number of gorgeous drinks that will look great in your social media feed. So break out those phones and set them to portrait mode.

STRAWBERRY MATCHA LATTE

It was a warm summer day in San Francisco, and we had a bunch of leftover puree from these incredible strawberries that we'd been playing with. We also have a huge sweet tooth, so we usually have a pack of Kit Kats (or Haribo gummy bears) on us. This particular day, the Kit Kats were Japanese and were green-tea-flavored. We took a bite of one right after tasting those strawberries. . . . You know when Remy in *Ratatouille* closes his eyes and the flavors explode in his imagination? *That*.

It took a while for people to understand the combination of strawberries, matcha, and milk, but it soon became one of our top drinks. Now it's beyond an icon. People have made cartoons out of it. A fan once turned it into a Halloween costume. We were in Japan just last year and saw a shop in Kyoto promoting a Strawberry Matcha Latte boba drink. When we asked the cashier about the origins of the drink, she said it's popular in America.

The key to the look of this drink is the viscosity levels, so the ratios, process, and sourcing must be followed to a T if you want that tricolored presentation. The strawberry puree shouldn't be perfectly smooth, but be more like applesauce. You want the matcha to start out super pasty, more like peanut butter than tea, and then get thinned out gradually by the water. Use a thermometer to gauge the temperature.

MAKES 1 GLASS

RECOMMENDED TOPPINGS: BOBA, GRASS JELLY, SAGO

1½ teaspoons matcha powder

3½ tablespoons filtered water, heated to 170°F

2 to 4 tablespoons toppings of your choice (optional)

3 ounces (¼ cup + 2 tablespoons) Strawberry Puree (recipe follows)

8 ounces (by weight) ice cubes

¾ cup whole milk

Place the matcha powder in a bowl and add 1 tablespoon of the hot water. Whisk vigorously to make a paste. It should have the consistency of peanut butter. Then add the remaining 2½ tablespoons hot water and whisk vigorously until any remaining clumps disappear.

Put the toppings, if using, in a large glass. Pour in the strawberry puree. Add the ice and the milk. Then gently pour the matcha over the ice milk, aiming for the ice cubes to keep the layers cleanly separated.

Hit the Ice

When you pour the matcha for the top layer, do it carefully, and always "hit the ice," as we say. Hitting the ice, instead of dropping the shot right in, gives the tea something to deflect against, slowing it down and spreading it in a clean horizontal layer. The good bobaristas always take the time to hit the ice.

strawberry puree

MAKES ABOUT 3 CUPS

1½ cups cold filtered water
1 cup raw cane sugar, preferably turbinado
2 cups fresh strawberries, hulled

Combine the water, sugar, and strawberries in a blender and blend until the mixture is pureed but still slightly chunky.

The puree will keep, refrigerated, for about a week.

The Boba Book

CARAMEL MATCHA LATTE

Caramel and matcha? That's a total mash-up! It's Meiji-era Japan meets Mars bars. It's a rural county fair meets antioxidant-food-trend city café. It really shouldn't be served cold, but for some reason it is, and it's just better that way.

As you do in many of our drinks, try to "hit the ice" (see page 105) with the matcha, pouring it straight onto the cubes. It helps disperse the drink evenly and slowly, and makes for a prettier presentation.

MAKES 1 GLASS

RECOMMENDED TOPPINGS: BOBA, MANGO PUDDING, EGG PUDDING

1½ teaspoons matcha powder

3½ tablespoons filtered water, heated to 170°F

¼ cup Pandan Caramel Sauce (recipe follows)

2 to 4 tablespoons toppings of your choice (optional)

8 ounces (by weight) ice cubes

¾ cup whole milk

Place the matcha powder in a bowl and add 2 teaspoons of the hot water. Whisk vigorously to make a paste. It should have the consistency of smooth peanut butter. Add the remaining hot water and whisk vigorously until any remaining clumps disappear.

Coat the inside of a glass with the caramel sauce (see page 55). Add the toppings, if using, the ice, and the milk. Then gently pour the matcha over the milk, aiming for the ice cubes to keep the layers cleanly separated.

pandan caramel sauce

Who doesn't love caramel sauce? This is a great one, with the addition of pandan.

This recipe makes a bunch. We figured you'll use this in some drinks in this book, and you'll want some left over because you seem like the kind of person who knows what to do with caramel sauce. Oh, wait, you don't? OK, let's see . . . Enjoy this on your ice cream sundaes, try some caramel-dipped green apples, or make caramel candies. That's just a few ideas to get the chips rolling. Feel free to get creative with it. Caramel-dipped bacon, anyone?

MAKES ABOUT 2 CUPS

½ cup filtered water

2 cups white sugar

1½ teaspoons sea salt

2 cups heavy whipping cream

1 tablespoon salted butter

2 teaspoons vanilla extract

¼ teaspoon pandan extract
(fresh leaves are hard to find,
and frozen are inconsistent)

In a small saucepan, combine the water, sugar, and salt. Bring to a boil over high heat and cook for about 12 minutes, until a golden to golden-brown color begins to show in the bubbles.

Slowly add the cream, being careful to avoid any spattering or the steam that will come up. Add the butter and the vanilla and pandan extracts. The sugar may seize (harden); if it does, turn the heat down to medium and stir the mixture continuously until it's all smooth again. Remove the pot from the heat and allow the sauce to cool.

Store the caramel sauce in the fridge for up to 2 weeks. When using it, bring the sauce up to room temperature or warm it in the microwave or over gentle heat on the stovetop.

Pandan custard is one of my all-time top desserts. I get it from this place Bhan Kanon Thai in Thai Town in L.A. But I've always struggled to describe pandan's flavor . . .

We like to say that pandan is a common flavor in Southeast Asian cuisine that is kind of like a mix of vanilla and Thai jasmine rice.

And that color . . .

It's a brilliant bright green! Unmistakable.

How to 'Gram Your Drink

We couldn't write a book without acknowledging one of our trade secrets. Boba Guys grew up in front of the public, on Instagram. We designed our first store around Instagram culture, so hm . . . this might be pandering, but we know y'all want this! Here are some basic tips to get a great shot.

Find a soft, indirect source of natural light.

Light from a window on a sunny day is good, but a cloudy day is often better! What you often want is light to be diffused—meaning you don't want the sun shining straight onto your drink, which makes for a sharp glare. You can draw blinds or curtains to help soften the light and create a buffer between the sun and your drink.

Try to make sure there's 3 to 5 feet of space between the drink and the wall behind it.

This will help create some separation between the drink and your backdrop, which always looks nice.

Try to find complementary or contrasting colors in your compositions.

For a green drink like our Matcha Mule, a shot of red or a deep orange might work nicely—for example, if you have a painting or poster in the background with those colors. Don't be shy about color-scheming your set a little, even if it's just your studio apartment.

Allow a cold drink to sit long enough that a little condensation starts to form on the glass.

It just looks cool.

Dress the set with a few things.

Have some leftover ingredients? Carefully set them around the drink to present them casually and aesthetically. Like if you're shooting the Strawberry Matcha Latte, some berries, some tea, and a small steel container of milk could fill out the frame nicely.

Shoot a ton.

Different angles, close-ups, wides, portrait mode, landscape mode. . . . It's digital. Go crazy.

Filter tastefully.

#nofilter is for showoffs. Boosting the brightness and saturation usually helps.

Specialty Drinks

JAPANESE COFFEE COLA

This recipe is based on one of our favorite drinks in Japan, the espresso coke from Coffee Elementary School in Tokyo introduced to us by one of our dear friends—and culture king—Eugene Hu. The combination of coffee and cola has been around for a while in Japan (coffee is an actual flavor of Coca-Cola there, like how we have Cherry Coke in the U.S.). It's acidic and sweet and effervescent, but has that coffee flavor complexity and extra kick. And then you get that smooth mouthfeel from the buttercream topping, which is our twist. It's like an American Coke Float. かんぱい Kanpai!

MAKES 1 GLASS

RECOMMENDED TOPPINGS: NONE

5 ounces (by weight) ice cubes

¼ cup Cold Brew Coffee (page 151)

1 cup cola, preferably one made with cane sugar

½ cup Salted Buttercream Topping (recipe follows)

Fill a glass with the ice and add the cold brew. Slowly pour the cola over the ice. Top with the buttercream topping. Mix before drinking.

salted buttercream topping

Brick toast, sweetened with condensed milk and served warm with a pat of butter, is a staple food you'll see in breakfast cafés everywhere in Hong Kong. We adapted its flavor for a perfect sweet-savory whipped topping for our drinks. We love that hit of salt with all the sweetness and creaminess, and it adds a bit of heft and body to the drink. It makes it more of a complete beverage—both filling and fun.

MAKES 6 TO 8 SERVINGS

3 tablespoons powdered sugar
1 cup heavy whipping cream
1 tablespoon salted butter
2 tablespoons sweetened condensed milk

Sift the powdered sugar into the bowl of a stand mixer. Add the heavy cream and attach the whisk attachment. Start the mixer on medium-low speed.

While the cream is whipping, melt the butter in a bowl in the microwave; it shouldn't take more than 20 or 30 seconds, maybe less. Once the butter is melted, thoroughly combine it with the condensed milk.

Continue whipping the cream, gradually increasing the speed to medium-high. Whip until the cream thickens and ripples start forming. Turn the mixer speed back down to medium-low and slowly add the condensed milk mixture. Continue mixing until the condensed milk is no longer visible, and stop the mixer when soft peaks form. In other words, it will look like whipped cream, but it will be soft, not stiff and fluffy. (Be sure to not overwhip it.)

Store the topping in an airtight container in the refrigerator for up to 7 days.

MARMALADE DRINKS

It's kind of mind-blowing how being outside without refrigeration is a key factor in how all street-side drinks developed in Asia.

Totally. That's why most boba shops came to make drinks with powders. They're shelf stable! Necessity is the mother of invention. It wasn't about being cheap!

Even though it's not common to use marmalades (of all kinds, not just orange) in drinks, there are reasons to do so. They're delicious. They're fully portable. We have a jar of Korean honey citron marmalade on hand at all times—great for hot teas and when you need to shut down a cough. They can sit on a shelf.

And we love marmalade drinks because they provide a platform—you can expand on them by adding fresh fruit, you can tweak the flavor base with other juices, and you can bring the acidity or sweetness up or down by combining it with other ingredients or adjusting the amount you use. It's the perfect drink to remix, as much a part of tradition as it is something completely new.

PEACHES AND CREAM

MAKES 1 GLASS

**RECOMMENDED TOPPINGS:
TAPIOCA CHIA SEED PUDDING, MATCHA PUDDING,
COCONUT ALMOND JELLY**

2 to 4 tablespoons toppings of your choice (optional)

¼ cup Roasted Peach Marmalade (recipe follows)

5 ounces (by weight) ice cubes

¾ cup filtered water

¼ cup Salted Buttercream Topping (page 113)

Put the toppings, if using, in a glass. Add the peach marmalade and the ice. Pour the water gently over the ice. Spoon the buttercream topping over the ice. Gently give your drink a stir to mix everything together before drinking.

roasted peach marmalade

MAKES 4 CUPS

1 pound frozen or fresh yellow peaches, sliced
(use fresh if you can)

1 tablespoon fresh lemon juice

1 cup filtered water

1 cup light brown sugar

2 cups white sugar

2 tablespoons dry pectin

½ tablespoon finely grated lemon zest

Preheat the oven to 350°F.

If you're using fresh peaches, bring a pot of water to a boil, drop the peaches in, and blanch for 10 seconds. Then transfer the peaches to a bowl of ice water. When they are cool enough to handle, peel off the skins. Pit the peaches and cut them into ½-inch cubes. If you're using frozen peaches, just thaw them.

Line a baking sheet with parchment paper and spread the peaches out evenly on the parchment. Roast for 10 to 15 minutes, until soft. Transfer the peaches to a medium-size pot. Add the lemon juice and water. Set the pot over medium-high heat and stir the peaches to prevent them from burning. Once the water begins to boil, add the brown sugar, white sugar, pectin, and lemon zest. Bring the mixture back up to a boil and let it boil for 1 minute. Then take the pot off the heat, allow to cool until warm, and for best results, use a regular blender or a stick blender to blend the contents together until smooth. Let the marmalade cool to room temperature, and store it in the fridge overnight to let it set up before using.

You can store the marmalade in the refrigerator for up to 2 weeks.

KIWI GUAVA MARMALADE TEA

MAKES 1 GLASS

RECOMMENDED TOPPINGS:
FRESCA KONJAC JELLY

2 to 4 tablespoons toppings of your choice
(optional)

¼ cup Kiwi Guava Marmalade
(recipe follows)

5 ounces (by weight) ice cubes

6 ounces filtered water

Put the toppings, if using, in a glass. Add
the kiwi guava marmalade and the ice.
Pour the water gently over the ice. Give
your drink a gentle stir to mix everything
together before drinking.

The Boba Book

kiwi guava marmalade

MAKES ABOUT 3 CUPS

5 kiwis

½ medium-size guava

½ cup store-bought lime juice
or the fresh-squeezed juice of 3 to 4 limes

1 cup filtered water

2 cups white sugar

2 tablespoons dry pectin

Remove the skin of the kiwis and the guava, and cut the fruit into quarters. In a small saucepan, combine the kiwis, guava, and lime juice with the water. Bring to a rolling boil over high heat. Add the sugar and pectin. Turn the heat down to medium and simmer until the fruit starts to break down, about 10 minutes. Then bring the mixture back up to a boil over high heat and let it boil for 1 minute. Take the pot off the heat, allow to cool until warm, and for the best results, use a standard blender or a stick blender to mix the contents together until smooth. Let the marmalade cool to room temperature, and chill it in the fridge overnight before serving.

Store the marmalade in the fridge for up to 2 weeks.

YUZU PEAR MARMALADE TEA

MAKES 1 GLASS

RECOMMENDED TOPPINGS: FRESCA KONJAC JELLY, GRASS JELLY

2 to 4 tablespoons toppings of your choice (optional)

¼ cup Yuzu Pear Marmalade (recipe follows)

5 ounces (by weight) ice cubes

6 ounces filtered water

Put the toppings, if using, in a glass. Add the marmalade and the ice. Pour the water gently over the ice. Gently give your drink a stir to mix everything together before drinking.

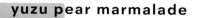

yuzu pear marmalade

MAKES ABOUT 3 CUPS

1¼ pounds Korean yellow pears
(Korean pears can be huge, so if you can,
weigh them out as you shop.)

3 cups filtered water

3 ounces (6 tablespoons) yuzu juice
(available at Asian markets or online)

½ tablespoon grated fresh ginger

1 teaspoon grated lemon zest

1½ cups white sugar

1½ tablespoons pectin

Peel the pears, core them, and cut the flesh into 1-inch cubes. In a small saucepan, combine the pear cubes, water, and yuzu juice. Bring the contents to a rolling boil over high heat. Turn the heat down to medium and simmer, stirring occasionally, until the pears have softened and two-thirds of the water has cooked away, about 12 minutes.

Add the ginger, lemon zest, sugar, and pectin to the pears. Bring the mixture back up to a boil over high heat and let it boil for 1 minute. Take the pot off the heat, let it cool until warm, and for best results, use a standard blender or a stick blender to blend it until smooth. Using a fine-mesh strainer, strain out the pear granules. Let the marmalade cool to room temperature. Store it in the fridge overnight before serving.

You can store the marmalade in the fridge for up to 2 weeks.

SPARKLING ROSE MATCHA

We've always experimented with Soda-Streams and effervescence, and we love the idea of sparkling teas. They're healthful, too. . . . They've got antioxidants!

> For two guys who live in S.F., I gotta say, you're sounding very L.A. right now.

> Well, we did make this recipe originally for our L.A. stores! It's for the culture, my man.

This floral, vegetal, bubbly pick-me-up is perfect for a hot afternoon. The matcha is pretty subtle in this one, so you don't get much of its bitterness and you can drink this all day long. You can find dried edible rose petals at specialty herb shops or online.

MAKES 1 GLASS

RECOMMENDED TOPPINGS: NONE

5 ounces (by weight) ice cubes

2 tablespoons Rose Syrup (recipe follows)

8 ounces sparkling water

3 tablespoons Matcha Cold Brew (recipe follows)

Add the ice, and then the rose syrup, to a glass. Slowly pour in the sparkling water. Gently pour the cold-brew matcha over the ice, aiming for the ice to help with the layering effect.

rose syrup

MAKES ABOUT 1½ CUPS

½ cup dried edible rose petals
1 cup filtered water, heated to 200°F
1 cup white sugar

Steep the dried rose petals in the hot water for 12 minutes.

Pour the sugar into a storage container. Strain the rose-infused water into the container. Mix thoroughly until the sugar has fully dissolved, and allow to cool.

Store the syrup in the fridge for up to 2 weeks.

matcha cold brew

MAKES ABOUT 1 CUP

1½ teaspoons matcha powder
7 ounces (¾ cup + 2 tablespoons) cold filtered water

Place the matcha powder in a bowl and add 2 tablespoons of the cold water. Whisk vigorously to make a thin paste. Then slowly add the remaining ¾ cup cold water and whisk vigorously until any clumps disappear.

MATCHA PALMER

The classic Arnold Palmer is lemonade and iced tea—standard iced tea, which usually means black tea. But Arnold Palmer played on the green, after all, so we think he'd appreciate a grassy matcha with his lemonade. We love to make our lemonade with Meyer lemons, which are a variety that is a cross between lemons and mandarin oranges; they have a less tart, slightly sweeter juice. If you just have regular lemons, it'll still be great (though you may want to add a little more sugar to balance the sourness). Or try the variation below using yuzu, the super-floral Japanese citrus.

You have to be *super* careful when layering this drink—make sure to "hit the ice" because there isn't a whole lot of density difference to keep the liquids separate.

MAKES 1 GLASS

RECOMMENDED TOPPINGS: TAPIOCA CHIA SEED PUDDING, FRESCA KONJAC JELLY

2 to 4 tablespoons toppings of your choice (optional)

5 ounces (by weight) ice cubes

4 ounces Lemonade (recipe follows)

7 ounces Matcha Cold Brew (page 121)

Put the toppings, if using, in a glass, and add the ice and the lemonade. Gently pour in the matcha cold brew, aiming for the ice cubes to create the layering effect.

lemonade

MAKES 2 CUPS

⅔ cup filtered water, cold or room temperature

⅔ cup freshly squeezed Meyer lemon juice (from 4 to 5 medium-size lemons)

⅔ cup white sugar

In a small pitcher, stir together the water, lemon juice, and sugar. Make sure the sugar has completely dissolved. Set aside or store in the fridge for up to a week.

VARIATION:

To make a yuzu lemonade, replace half the lemon juice with yuzu juice.

STRAWBERRY JASMINE TEA FRESCA

This is an ideal early summer drink. It's floral and light and market-fresh. If the Strawberry Matcha Latte is like a hoppy IPA, this is like a refreshing Kölsch. When the berries start to show up at the farmer's market in the late spring, we recommend getting a flat. You'll be drinking a lot of these as the days grow long, from Memorial Day through the dog days of August.

MAKES 1 GLASS

RECOMMENDED TOPPINGS: FRESCA KONJAC JELLY, MANGO PUDDING

⅓ cup Strawberry Puree (make as on page 106, but puree until fully smooth)

2 to 4 tablespoons toppings of your choice (optional)

5 ounces (by weight) ice cubes

⅓ cup Iced Jasmine Tea (recipe follows)

⅓ cup cold filtered water

Pour the strawberry puree into a glass. Add the toppings, if using, and the ice. Gently pour in the tea, aiming for the ice to layer the tea above the puree. Then gently pour in the water, aiming for the ice to create another layer.

iced jasmine tea

MAKES 1 CUP

2 tablespoons jasmine tea leaves

5 ounces (½ cup + 2 tablespoons) filtered water, heated to 170°F

4 ounces (by weight) ice cubes

Steep the tea leaves in the hot water for 4 minutes.

Fill a glass with the ice cubes and strain the tea over the ice. Allow the ice to fully melt.

RASPBERRY PINEAPPLE TEA FRESCA

Tropical but hefty, floral and refreshing, this tea fresca is a guaranteed crowd-pleaser.

MAKES 1 GLASS

RECOMMENDED TOPPINGS: FRESCA KONJAC JELLY

⅓ cup Raspberry Pineapple Puree (recipe follows)

2 to 4 tablespoons toppings of your choice (optional)

5 ounces (by weight) ice cubes

⅓ cup Iced Jasmine Tea (page 125)

⅓ cup cold filtered water

Pour the puree into a glass. Add the toppings, if using, and the ice. Gently pour in the tea, aiming for the ice to layer the tea above the puree. Then gently add the water, aiming for the ice to create another layer.

raspberry pineapple puree

MAKES 3 CUPS

1½ cups filtered water

1 cup raw cane sugar, preferably turbinado

1 cup fresh raspberries

1 cup diced pineapple (preferably fresh, but frozen—and thawed—will do)

In a blender, combine the water, sugar, raspberries, and pineapple. Blend until fully pureed and smooth.

Store the puree in an airtight container in the fridge for up to 1 week.

MANGO MATCHA FRESCA

We feel that with the long association of Japanese and Hawai'ian cultures, we couldn't have been the first to mix mango and matcha. This drink is sweet and tangy, and since we are using fresh mango, it has that creamy texture, too. The matcha brings an astringency and a grassy quality that plays the perfect foil to the out-and-out mango attack. This drink is guaranteed to brighten your day, even if you live in the sunny climes of Southern California.

MAKES 1 GLASS

RECOMMENDED TOPPINGS: FRESCA KONJAC JELLY

½ cup Mango Puree (page 65)

2 to 4 tablespoons toppings of your choice (optional)

5 ounces (by weight) ice cubes

7 ounces Matcha Cold Brew (page 121)

Pour the puree into a glass, and add the toppings, if using, and then the ice. Gently pour in the matcha cold brew, aiming for the ice cubes to help layer the matcha cold brew at the top of the drink.

STRAWBERRY CALI-PICO

Calpico is a Japanese drink that we say is like a yogurt soda, but that doesn't come close to capturing how delicious it is. The sourness and fattiness of the yogurt make it next-level as a soda. It's sweet and tart. It should be as iconic as Coke, and it is in lots of Asian communities. We used to sneak it into our parents' grocery baskets at the local 99 Ranch Market. Couldn't get enough. That was 25 years ago, and none of our non-Asian friends drank it. Of course, now that fermented things and gut health are catching on in the West, we're seeing Calpico more and more.

Don't laugh, but we need to tell you that Calpico is normally known as Calpis in Japan. It is pronounced the way you think it sounds. And for trivia geeks, Calpis is owned by Asahi, the beer company.

Interesting . . .

We just don't want you wandering Japan by yourself asking if Calpis and Calpico are the same. We share because we care!

We use kefir, basically a drinkable yogurt, to make our version of Calpico, and we mix it with jasmine tea, fresh berries, and sparking water. You may have to go to an Asian supermarket to find Calpico, but you can make this version from ingredients you can find at any conventional grocery store in the U.S., no matter where you are.

MAKES 1 GLASS

RECOMMENDED TOPPINGS: BOBA

⅓ cup Strawberry Puree (page 106)

2 to 4 tablespoons toppings of your choice (optional)

5 ounces (by weight) ice cubes

⅓ cup Iced Jasmine Tea (page 125)

⅓ cup sparkling water

⅓ cup kefir or drinkable yogurt

Pour the strawberry puree into a glass. Add the toppings, if using, and the ice. Gently pour in the jasmine tea, aiming for the ice cubes to help layer the tea above the puree. Repeat the layering process with the sparkling water. Then layer in the kefir, aiming for the ice cubes to create an even layer.

limeade

MAKES 5 CUPS

1 cup fresh lime juice (from 6 to 8 limes)

2 or 3 fresh shiso leaves (or 6 to 8 mint leaves), shredded (optional)

1 cup white sugar

4 cups filtered water, room temperature or slightly warm

In a pitcher, stir together the lime juice and the shiso or mint leaves.

In a small mixing bowl, combine the sugar with the water, stirring until all the sugar is dissolved. (If the sugar doesn't all dissolve, you can heat the mixture in a large saucepan over low heat and whisk until it's fully dissolved. Allow it to cool to room temperature.)

Add the sugar water to the pitcher and stir. Set the limeade aside or store it in the fridge for up to a week.

CHAMANGO OR WATERMELON CHAMOY

This drink is all about the irresistible Mexican combination of spices, chile, and seasonings with fresh fruit. It's salty, it's spicy, it's got acidity from the lime, herbaciousness from the shiso, and the bright freshness and sweetness of mango or watermelon (take your pick).

Tajín is the chile-lime powder that's omnipresent in the corner stores of pretty much any neighborhood where there is a Mexican community. It's a brand, actually, but also a catchall term for the spicy-tart mixtures commonly sprinkled on top of fresh-cut fruit sold on the street, and it adds an unmistakable flavor to a *michelada*—the tomato/spice/beer shandy from Mexico.

Chamoy is another Mexican ingredient. It comes in lots of forms, from a paste to a candy to a sauce, and is basically a salted, pickled, sour fruit thing, often made from plums. It's used commonly in chamoyada, which is a Mexican shaved-ice dessert. So, you know we're all about bridging cultures, and we right away saw a bridge from chamoy and chamoyada to Japanese fermented ume plums (see page 98) and Asian shaved ices. You can also find chamoy drinks in grocery stores all over California.

It turns out, though, that food historians think that chamoy actually came to Mexico with Chinese immigrants, and is from the same family tree as pickled ume! So it's a full-circle bridging cultures thing. And this drink is our homage to all that deliciousness: a Tajín and chamoy-spiked limeade, blended with shiso and mango or watermelon. It's sweet, sour, spicy, and it feels like our home in the Mission District of San Francisco.

MAKES 2 GLASSES

**RECOMMENDED TOPPINGS:
SAGO, FRESCA KONJAC JELLY**

1 pound mango
or watermelon flesh,
coarsely chopped

7 ounces (by weight)
ice cubes

½ cup Limeade
(recipe opposite)

1 tablespoon Tajín seasoning
(chile-lime powder)

½ cup apricot chamoy
sauce (available at Latin
groceries)

2 to 4 tablespoons (per glass)
toppings of your choice
(optional)

In a blender, combine the mango or watermelon, ice cubes, limeade, and ½ tablespoon of the Tajín seasoning. Blend until the ice is crushed and everything is mixed.

Coat the inside of 2 glasses with some of the chamoy sauce. Carefully layer each glass with half of the blended drink, the toppings, if using, and the remaining chamoy sauce on top. Garnish the top of each drink with the remaining Tajín powder.

LI HING MUI PINEAPPLE MANGO COCONUT DRINK

Li hing mui, another salted, dried plum product, is a popular seasoning used in Hawai'i and across Asia. It's a little sweet and salty and sour. It's good with tropical fruits especially, like pineapple and guava—the saltiness balances their sugars and the added tanginess makes the flavors pop, like fruit in HD. It's perfect. You can find li hing mui at most Asian markets, and at local "crack seed" stores in Hawai'i.

Li hing mui is super potent and salty. You don't want to use more than, say, the salt you would use to rim a margarita glass. In this drink, we use it to flavor mango and pineapple, and the coconut gives it all a delicious richness. We've been seeing it show up in fancy cocktails in the U.S. beyond Hawai'i, which we love. We'd love to see it in more places, like in spice rubs for meat.

Pro tip: You can also make this puree without the sugar and use it as a drizzle on ice cream. That's really good.

MAKES 1 GLASS

RECOMMENDED TOPPINGS: SAGO, BOBA, FRESCA KONJAC JELLY

1 tablespoon li hing mui powder (dried salted plum powder), or as needed

¼ cup Li Hing Mui Pineapple Mango Puree (recipe follows)

2 to 4 tablespoons toppings of your choice (optional)

5 ounces (by weight) ice cubes

1 cup coconut beverage (you can find this at stores like Trader Joe's; it's essentially coconut milk thinned down to a drinkable consistency)

1 tablespoon finely chopped fresh mango

Put the li hing mui powder in a small dish. Wet the rim of a glass and dip it into the li hing mui, as though you're salting the rim of a margarita glass. (Reserve the excess for another use.) Coat the inside of the glass with some of the pineapple mango puree (see page 55). Fill the bottom of the glass with the remaining puree. Add the toppings, if using, and the ice. Slowly pour the coconut beverage over the ice, aiming for the ice cubes to create a layering effect. Garnish the top of the drink with the chopped mangoes.

li hing mui pineapple mango puree

MAKES ABOUT 2½ CUPS

1 cup diced fresh mango

1 cup diced pineapple (preferably fresh, but frozen—and thawed—will do)

1 cup white sugar

1 cup filtered water

½ tablespoon li hing mui powder

In a blender, combine the mango, pineapple, sugar, water, and li hing mui powder. Blend until everything is smooth.

This will keep in the fridge for up to 1 week.

PINK DRINK

On Wednesdays, we drink pink.

This drink was made for Instagram. It's that "millennial pink" look . . . and it slays. It drips . . . literally. Okay, we have no idea what we just said, but pink drinks have been all the rage over the last few years, so we had to slip one in here like a Post Malone feature.

We took inspiration from our friends at Alfred Tea, a local Southern California chain. They get a deep pink color from beets. We opted for a berry base as we prefer a fruitier drink profile for this. We figure if you're going to 'Gram this drink for fifteen minutes, you need something refreshing after you're done! (In the old days, we used to serve this with a shot of matcha on top. It's delicious!)

MAKES 1 GLASS

**RECOMMENDED TOPPINGS:
BOBA**

¼ cup Strawberry
Raspberry Puree
(recipe follows)

2 to 4 tablespoons toppings
of your choice (optional)

5 ounces (by weight)
ice cubes

¾ cup almond milk
Horchata (see page 67),
made with high-quality,
extra-rich almond milk like
Califia Farms or Elmhurst
Milked Almonds instead of
dairy milk

Pour the puree into a glass, and add the toppings, if using, and the ice. Pour in the horchata, aiming for the ice cubes to create a layering effect. Mix before drinking.

---

strawberry raspberry puree

MAKES 2 CUPS

5 fresh medium strawberries, hulled

½ cup fresh raspberries

½ cup white sugar

1 cup filtered water

Combine the strawberries, raspberries, sugar, and water in a blender, and blend until smooth.

The puree will keep, refrigerated, for up to 1 week.

UBE HALAYA SMOOTHIE

There's a famous Filipino dessert called *halaya*. It's super delicious, almost like a pudding, and it's made with mashed purple yams. We have a lot of Filipino staff members at Boba Guys and we worked really hard to make a drink that honors the tradition of halaya. We think this does it—it's creamy and rich, coconutty and vanilla-y, and has the sweet, nutty taste of ube.

Ube, the purple yam in halaya, and taro, the sweet-potato-like root in lots of Chinese dishes and desserts, are common flavors in boba shops. But they're almost always represented by powders and dyes. We make our drinks with the real ingredients, and ube might amaze you with its bright, brilliant purple color, no dyes needed. Nature is enough!

MAKES 1 GLASS

RECOMMENDED TOPPINGS: BOBA, GRASS JELLY, EGG PUDDING

¼ cup Ube Jam (recipe follows)

¾ cup coconut beverage (you can find this at stores like Trader Joe's; it's essentially coconut milk thinned down to a drinkable consistency)

5 ounces (by weight) ice cubes

2 to 4 tablespoons toppings of your choice (optional)

Combine the ube jam, coconut beverage, and ice in a blender, and blend on medium speed until there are no visible clumps.

Spoon the toppings, if using, into a glass, pour in the ube shake, and serve.

Alternatively, you can serve the drink "on the rocks": Put the ube jam, toppings if using, and ice in a glass. Gently pour the coconut beverage over the ice, aiming for the ice cubes to help it layer evenly. Stir with a spoon before drinking.

ube jam

MAKES ABOUT 1½ CUPS

⅓ pound ube (purple yam)
⅓ cup filtered water
⅔ cup white sugar
1 tablespoon vanilla extract

Using a fork, puncture the length of the ube(s) on two sides. Microwave the ube for 8 to 10 minutes, until soft, and then allow it to cool until you can handle it. Remove the skin and put the flesh into a small saucepan. Add the water and turn the heat to high. Using a wooden spoon, mash the ube in the water until a thick mashed-potato-like paste forms. Stir in the sugar and vanilla extract, and mix until everything is well incorporated and there are no visible clumps. Remove the pan from the heat and allow the jam to cool. (For maximum smoothness, you can blend the jam in a blender.)

The jam will keep in the fridge for up to 1 week.

HAW FLAKES TEA

It's hard for us to think of childhood without thinking of Haw Flakes: the sweet, tangy, pink-colored fruit candy disks. When we were kids, they came in tiny packs with dyed red wrapping and a label design that never exited the 1940s. A pack of Haw Flakes wasn't much bigger than a stack of quarters, so you could easily stash one in your pocket or lunch bag. Most days if you did a pat-down on us, you'd find Haw Flakes somewhere. And they were a constant source of frustration—you could never eat that top disk in a Haw Flakes pack because the paper always stuck to it.

Sounds like they're kind of the Asian Necco Wafer.

When you're a kid in a Taiwanese/Chinese family, you're used to being served bitter herb soups that some auntie says are supposed to be good for your health. That's what the *kam chou* part of this drink nods to. It's a root that's similar in taste to licorice. It wouldn't be the only element of these soups—kam chou has a mellow, sweet flavor that's not bitter at all—but it was an unmistakable part. One of the best covert uses of Haw Flakes when you're a kid is to chase your sips of bitter herbal soup with your private stash of Haw Flakes. And turns out that kam chou and Haw Flakes are a banging flavor combination. So this drink is a tribute to that childhood ritual.

MAKES 8 GLASSES

**RECOMMENDED TOPPINGS:
BOBA**

½ cup Haw Flakes

½ cup plum juice or filtered water

12 cups (3 quarts) filtered water

¾ cup kam chou (look for this in Asian markets with a Chinese focus)

1½ cups white sugar

Ice, for serving

2 to 4 tablespoons (per glass) toppings of your choice (optional)

In a small mixing bowl, soak the Haw Flakes in the plum juice for 20 minutes.

In a medium-size pot, bring the filtered water to a boil over high heat. Add the soaked Haw Flakes with their soaking liquid, and add the kam chou. Cook, covered, at a rolling boil, for 1 hour, adding some more water if necessary to keep it from getting too reduced.

Strain out and discard the Haw Flakes and kam chou. Add the sugar to the strained liquid and boil, uncovered, for another 10 minutes, or until it has reduced to about 8 cups (2 quarts). (Or, if necessary, add water to reach this level.) Remove the pot from the heat and allow the tea to cool. Serve the drink over ice, with toppings, if desired.

Store the tea in a pitcher in the fridge for up to 5 days.

BUTTERFLY PEA AKA BANTHA MILK

Chances are, since you are reading this in the English language, you probably have never heard of butterfly pea and bantha milk.

OK, so we kind of made up "bantha milk," at least here on Earth, so you definitely haven't heard of it. But butterfly pea tea is real.

Ever since we were introduced to the butterfly pea flower, we knew we wanted to work with it, because it makes drinks with a gorgeous blue color. (Very few edible things are naturally blue. Think about it!)

It tastes a little like a cross between chamomile and green tea. Or almost like a Thai tea base, somewhat earthy and floral at the same time.

In traditional Chinese and Ayurvedic medicines, butterfly pea is known variously for being an anti-anxiety aid, a memory enhancer, an aphrodisiac . . . it's even purported to prevent hair loss! And while it has this long history in Asia, we didn't start to see a lot of butterfly pea until Instagram. All of a sudden our feeds were crowded with these bright blue lemonades.

Of course, as nerds, we love *Star Wars*. So we were re-re-watching *The Last Jedi* one night together, and we saw Luke drinking "bantha milk," which also has that same blue color. (Bantha, for those who are not nerds, is a fictional *Star Wars* animal that kind of looks like an elephant.) And we knew we had to make this fictional drink real. We mix the butterfly pea tea with a base of black tea and enrich it with sweetened condensed milk.

MAKES 1 GLASS

RECOMMENDED TOPPINGS: BOBA

1 tablespoon sweetened condensed milk

2 to 4 tablespoons toppings of your choice (optional)

5 ounces (by weight) ice cubes

1 cup Butterfly Pea Tea (recipe follows)

2½ ounces (¼ cup + 1 tablespoon) half-and-half

Coat the inside of a glass with the condensed milk (see page 55). Add the toppings, if using, and the ice. Pour the tea over the ice. Then pour the half-and-half in slowly, aiming for the ice to create a clean layer. Stir to mix before drinking.

butterfly pea tea

MAKES ABOUT 8 CUPS

6 tablespoons Ceylon black tea leaves

6 tablespoons dried butterfly pea flowers
(available online)

1 cup white sugar

6 cups filtered water, heated to 190°F

20 ounces (by weight) ice cubes

In a small mixing bowl, stir together the Ceylon tea
leaves, butterfly pea flowers, and sugar. Steep the
tea mixture in the hot water for 20 minutes.

Fill a pitcher with the ice and strain the tea over
the ice. Set the pitcher aside to allow the ice to fully
melt. Store it in the fridge for up to a week.

ICED PUMPKIN TURMERIC LATTE

OK, yes, the pumpkin spice latte is a cliché. So why are we doing one? Well, first of all, this isn't a pumpkin-*spice* latte, which is really about the spice mix *called* "pumpkin spice." Our version has real pumpkin in it for a natural, complex flavor, *and* a bunch of spices. But since we are doing "drinks of the world" here, we have to be real. Love it or hate it, PSL is one of the most iconic drinks of the world! So we just tried to spiff it up, Boba Guys–style. For this, we make a sweet-spiced pumpkin "jam," boosted with the earthiness of turmeric, and turn that into a drink with coconut milk.

> So when I order it, will the bobarista misspell my name on the cup?

> Of course not, Rorchart!

MAKES 1 GLASS

RECOMMENDED TOPPINGS: BOBA

¼ cup Spiced Pumpkin Turmeric Jam (recipe opposite)

¾ cup coconut beverage (you can find this at stores like Trader Joe's; it's essentially coconut milk thinned down to a drinkable consistency)

2 to 4 tablespoons toppings of your choice (optional)

8 ounces (by weight) ice cubes

In a blender, combine the pumpkin jam and the coconut beverage. Blend on medium speed until there are no visible clumps.

Put the toppings, if using, and the ice in a glass, and pour the pumpkin-coconut mixture over the ice.

spiced pumpkin turmeric jam

MAKES ABOUT 1½ CUPS

1 cup (8 ounces) canned pumpkin
(or fresh pumpkin; see note)

1 cup white sugar

1 tablespoon vanilla extract

1 teaspoon ground turmeric

1 teaspoon ground cinnamon

½ teaspoon ground cloves

½ teaspoon ground nutmeg

In a large saucepan, combine the pumpkin, sugar, vanilla extract, turmeric, cinnamon, cloves, and nutmeg, stirring until everything is well incorporated. Let it simmer over medium heat for a couple of minutes to infuse the flavors. Remove the pan from the heat and allow to cool.

The jam will keep in the refrigerator for up to 1 week.

NOTE:

If you're using fresh pumpkin, dice 8 ounces of pumpkin into ½-inch pieces. Place the diced pumpkin in a microwave-safe dish and cover it with plastic wrap. Microwave the pumpkin for 3 to 5 minutes, until it is soft/tender. Puree the pumpkin in a blender, adding water as necessary to keep it moving, and proceed as instructed.

COFFEE TEA MINT MOJITO

This is our homage to Philz Coffee, the venerable S.F. coffee chain, and their iconic beverage, the Mint Mojito, a creamy coffee with mint. We love Philz drinks, and love what they've done in coffee, a little similar to what we want to do in tea and boba. In the tradition vs. remix debate, Philz is on the side that values remixing. Even today, a coffee mint mojito sounds like it's from the future. So this is our version, in which we trade most of the coffee for tea, adding a subtle hit of fresh mint.

If you want to riff on this and add a warm spice note, almost like an eggnog spin, try simmering the syrup for a few minutes with a whole nutmeg and a couple of cardamom pods.

MAKES 1 GLASS

RECOMMENDED TOPPINGS: FRESCA KONJAC JELLY, GRASS JELLY

Leaves from 1 sprig fresh mint

¼ cup House Syrup (page 27)

2 to 4 tablespoons toppings of your choice (optional)

5 ounces (by weight) ice cubes

6 ounces (¾ cup) Brewed Boba Guys' Black Tea (page 27)

2 ounces (¼ cup) Cold Brew Coffee (page 151)

2½ ounces (¼ cup + 1 tablespoon) half-and-half or oat milk

In a large glass, use a muddler or a spoon to smash the mint leaves. Add the syrup, the toppings, if using, and the ice. Pour in the black tea, cold brew, and half-and-half. Mix before drinking.

CARAMEL ICED MILK

Our master recipe for Pandan Caramel Sauce (page 109) as a topping makes a large quantity. This is one of the easiest, most delicious ways to deal with your extra caramel sauce—just mix it with cold milk and drink away!

We first fell in love with this drink at Half and Half Tea House, which has a bunch of locations in the L.A. area. In fact, we're in love with a lot of their sweet drinks. It seems simple, but their focus on flavoring sweetened milks inspires us—their honey milk drink is classic. And then we started seeing other iterations of this idea, like a "black sugar boba" drink in Taipei: no tea, just boba, syrup, and milk. So this is our version of that.

MAKES 1 GLASS

RECOMMENDED TOPPINGS: BOBA, MATCHA PUDDING, EGG PUDDING

¼ cup Pandan Caramel Sauce (page 109)

2 to 4 tablespoons toppings of your choice (optional)

5 ounces (by weight) ice cubes

1 cup whole milk

Coat the inside of a glass with the caramel (see page 55). Add the toppings if using, the ice, and the milk. Stir before drinking.

COCONUT CHAI TEA

Be warned: Your house is going to smell very good when you're making this—spicy like clove, cardamom, and allspice, nutty and warm. There's nothing quite like these deeply aromatic flavors of India.

Like so many of the tea drinks from around the world that we take inspiration from, chai is typically served with milk. So we figured why not try a bulletproof riff, using coconut as the substitute? The coconut cream and coconut oil give the drink a lot of flavor and richness, and it froths and foams beautifully.

This recipe is also a chance for you to break out that mortar and pestle you got from your aunt three birthdays ago. But don't worry about being too precise with the pulverizing—you're going to be straining everything out before you drink. (You can also use a spice grinder or a food processor if auntie didn't provide.) This is a classic conversation tea. Have friends over for a cup and they'll ask you a lot of questions about how you did it.

MAKES 1 SERVING (HOT OR ICED)

RECOMMENDED TOPPINGS: BOBA, EGG PUDDING

1½ cups brewed Chai Tea Blend (page 62), hot
1 tablespoon coconut oil
1 tablespoon unsweetened coconut cream
Sweetener, as desired
2 to 4 tablespoons toppings of your choice (optional)
5 ounces (by weight) ice cubes (optional)

In a glass, combine the hot tea, coconut oil, and coconut cream. Sweeten, to taste. Stir thoroughly with a spoon so the oil is incorporated into the hot mixture.

Serve this hot or iced, with toppings as desired. If serving it iced, allow the tea to cool to room temperature before pouring it over the ice.

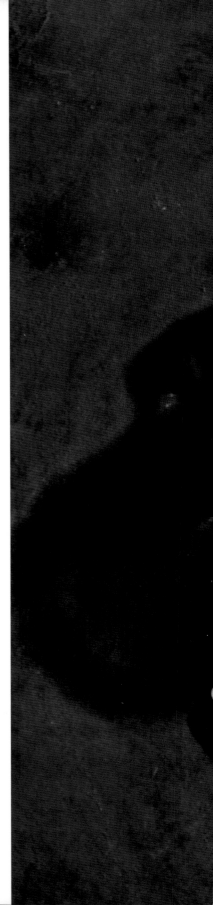

"DIRTY" HORCHATA

Boba Guys came up in the Mission District of San Francisco. We had our first pop-ups in the Mission and it's still our favorite store of all. The Mission District is a historically Hispanic neighborhood that has gentrified, but there is still a really strong presence of the old Mission—great taquerias and street food along with the newer businesses and restaurants. We met as employees at Timbuk2, the awesome S.F. bag company that's based there. And as many times as we left the office for boba breaks together, we also were crushing super burritos with spicy salsa verde and washing it all down with cinnamony, nutty, rice-milky horchata.

But, of course, right alongside those taquerias now are new-school coffee shops. So this drink is our love letter to the Mission: the one that used to be and the one that's there today. It's a classic well-made horchata. And it's dirtied up with a hit of new-school coffee.

> We should clarify that "dirty" in the cafe industry is an endearing term used when you put a shot of espresso over a drink. Like a Dirty Chai.

> They use that term in bartending, too.

> Okay, we're just overexplaining it then!

> We could have just named it something less provocative.

MAKES 1 GLASS

RECOMMENDED TOPPINGS: BOBA, GRASS JELLY, BLACK STICKY RICE, COCONUT ALMOND JELLY

2 to 4 tablespoons toppings of your choice (optional)

5 ounces (by weight) ice cubes

¾ cup Horchata (page 67)

¼ cup Cold Brew Coffee (recipe follows)

Put the toppings, if using, in a glass and add the ice. Pour in the horchata, and then gently pour the cold brew over the ice, aiming for the ice cubes to layer the cold brew on the top of the drink.

Making cold brew at home is one of the best ways to save money you'd otherwise spend at the café. And you don't have to buy a trillion-dollar espresso machine to do it!

cold brew coffee

We're not just a boba shop—we're a café, too. And to be a good café, you have to have a good cold brew. For the uninitiated, cold brew is like hot-brewed coffee with the acidity zapped out of it. It's a totally different representation of the bean. And it's super easy to make. You just need beans, water, refrigeration, and time. We use cold brew in a bunch of recipes, but you can also just drink this on its own. And if you love the flavor of it, you can even heat up your cold brew and enjoy it hot!

MAKES 8 CUPS

8 ounces coffee beans of your choice
5 cups filtered water, room temperature or cold
4 cups cold filtered water

Grind the coffee beans on the French press setting—i.e., a coarse grind. Put the grounds and the 5 cups water into a large container or bowl, and stir. Let steep at room temperature for 12 to 18 hours.

Pour the steeped coffee into a pitcher, straining out the grounds. The liquid is your concentrate. Add the 4 cups cold filtered water to this coffee concentrate, or dilute it to taste.

You can store the cold brew in the refrigerator for up to 7 days. You can also store the concentrate and dilute it to order.

SOUL MATÉ

We love maté, the South American tea that's traditionally drunk out of a dried-out gourd with a *bombilla*, a pipelike straw with a metal lip. It's a cool ritual. Maté is very strong, astringent, and vegetal, leaning toward bitter, earthy, and highly caffeinated. It should be as big around the world as matcha, but it hasn't quite caught on . . . yet.

We really wanted to make a milk tea from maté. We think it works on very much the same level as matcha. Maté's stronger flavor, though, means that we like to use half-and-half instead of milk to help balance the flavor.

MAKES 1 GLASS

RECOMMENDED TOPPINGS: BOBA

2 to 4 tablespoons toppings of your choice (optional)

5 ounces (by weight) ice cubes

2 ounces (¼ cup) House Syrup (page 27)

8 ounces (1 cup) Brewed Yerba Maté Tea (recipe follows)

2½ ounces (¼ cup + 1 tablespoon) half-and-half (or substitute other milk options like oat milk, almond milk, etc.)

Fill a glass with the toppings, if using, and the ice. Add the syrup and pour the tea over the ice. Add the half-and-half and stir until everything is mixed.

---

brewed yerba maté tea

MAKES ABOUT 1 CUP

2 tablespoons yerba maté tea leaves

½ cup + 2 tablespoons filtered water, heated to 190°F

4 ounces (by weight) ice cubes

Steep the tea leaves in the hot water for 4 minutes.

In a glass, strain the tea over the ice, and set the glass aside to allow the ice to fully melt.

CRÈME BRÛLÉE MATCHA LATTE

I remember I met you guys there and I ordered it. It looked like camouflage in a cup!

What's cool about it is that, as opposed to a lot of our drinks, Fluffy Head's layering is intentionally nonuniform. It doesn't have to be pristine to be beautiful!

We look at a lot—*a lot*—of pictures of drinks on Instagram; so honestly, it takes something pretty special to wow us. The first time we saw a post of a crème brûlée matcha latte definitely qualifies. We never saw one in person, though, until we went to a great drinks shop in downtown L.A. called Little Fluffy Head Café. Theirs is fantastic—a milky cold matcha swirled through with rich egg-custard sauce. This is our homage to that drink.

MAKES 1 GLASS

RECOMMENDED TOPPINGS: BOBA, CHÈ BA MÀU JELLY, EGG PUDDING

1½ teaspoons matcha powder

4 tablespoons filtered water, heated to 170°F

¼ cup Crème Brûlée Sauce (recipe follows)

1 tablespoon Vanilla Syrup (page 159)

2 to 4 tablespoons toppings of your choice (optional)

8 ounces (by weight) ice cubes

¾ cup whole milk

Place the matcha powder in a bowl and add 1 tablespoon of the hot water. Whisk vigorously to make a paste. It should have the consistency of peanut butter with no clumps. Add the remaining 3 tablespoons hot water and whisk vigorously until any remaining clumps disappear. Set the matcha aside.

Coat the inside of a glass with a good amount of the crème brûlée sauce. Layer the bottom of the glass with the remaining crème brûlée sauce. Add the syrup. Add the toppings, if using, the ice, and the milk. Then gently pour the matcha over the milk, aiming for the ice cubes to keep the layers cleanly separated. Mix before drinking.

The Boba Book

crème brûlée sauce

MAKES ABOUT 2 CUPS

3 large egg yolks at room temperature

¼ cup white sugar

2 tablespoons light brown sugar

½ teaspoon vanilla extract

1½ cups heavy whipping cream

½ cup whole milk

In a medium-size mixing bowl, prepare an ice bath by filling it with cold water and ice

In a small mixing bowl, whisk together the egg yolks, white sugar, brown sugar, and vanilla extract until the mixture thickens to a ribbon consistency; you'll see the distinct trails the whisk leaves behind for a moment before the mixture comes back together.

In a small saucepan, heat the cream and milk together over medium-high heat until steaming hot but not boiling. Remove the pan from the heat and slowly pour about a third of the hot cream mixture into the egg yolk mixture, whisking as you pour. When well mixed, whisk the contents of the bowl back into the saucepan. Cook over medium heat, stirring constantly, for 6 minutes or until the contents thicken into something like a custard—thicker than condensed milk but thinner than frosting. Remove the pan from the heat, and using a strainer to catch any overcooked egg bits, pour the contents into a bowl. Place the bowl in the ice bath to cool the sauce.

You can store the cooled sauce in the fridge for up to 3 days.

LONDON FOG

London Fog is a perfect name for what this drink is: a cloudy milk tea seasoned with vanilla. But by making this drink with Earl Grey tea, you get a whole new flavor, too. Bergamot oil gives Earl Grey its flowery citrus notes along with the Assam or Ceylon black tea base. There's nothing like it.

For the best flavor, use a small paring knife to slit open a vanilla bean and scrape out the tiny seeds. You can use the rest of the bean to steep and flavor other things, or submerge it in sugar to make vanilla sugar.

MAKES 1 LARGE CUP HOT TEA

RECOMMENDED TOPPINGS: BOBA

2 tablespoons Earl Grey tea leaves

7 ounces (¾ cup + 2 tablespoons) filtered water, heated to 190°F

6 ounces (¾ cup) whole milk or almond milk

2 to 4 tablespoons toppings of your choice (optional)

¼ teaspoon seeds from a vanilla bean, or ½ teaspoon vanilla extract

1 tablespoon House Syrup (page 27), or to taste

Steep the tea leaves in the hot water for 4 minutes.

Meanwhile, using the steam wand of an espresso machine, steam the milk until it begins to foam. (If you don't have a steamer, you can cook the milk in a small saucepan over medium heat, stirring, until the milk starts frothing, about 3 minutes.)

Place the toppings, if using, in a large cup or a mug, strain the hot tea into it, and add the frothed milk. While the tea is still hot, add the vanilla. Add the syrup and stir.

MATCHA COFFEE

We based this drink on the famous "military latte" at Sawada, a Japanese café with locations in Chicago and New York. The military latte is a beautiful drink of espresso, matcha, and milk, so named because the colors come together to almost look like military camo. Hiroshi Sawada, the renowned latte artist, popularized this drink in his cafés, and they are definitely a modern classic.

For a perfect version of this drink, you'll want to use a coffee that has berry notes and a sweet roasted flavor, to match the matcha's vegetal-ness and the smooth milk. This has the flavor benefits of both coffee and tea. It's having your coffee—and drinking your tea, too!

MAKES 1 LARGE CUP HOT LATTE

RECOMMENDED TOPPINGS: BOBA, EGG PUDDING, BLACK STICKY RICE

½ tablespoon matcha powder

4 tablespoons filtered water, heated to 170°F

1 to 2 tablespoons toppings of your choice (optional)

2 ounces freshly pulled espresso

6 ounces whole milk

1 tablespoon Vanilla Syrup (recipe follows)

1 teaspoon unsweetened cocoa powder

Place the matcha powder in a bowl and add 1 tablespoon of the hot water. Whisk vigorously to make a paste. It should have the consistency of peanut butter with no clumps. Add the remaining 3 tablespoons hot water and whisk vigorously, until any remaining clumps disappear.

Strain the matcha into a large cup or a mug. Add the toppings, if using, and the espresso. Steam or heat the milk to 140°F, and gently pour the warm milk into the espresso-matcha mixture. Add the syrup and sift the cocoa powder over the latte. Mix together before drinking.

vanilla syrup

MAKES ABOUT 2½ CUPS

1 cup dark brown sugar

1 cup white sugar

1 tablespoon vanilla bean paste or extract

1¼ cups filtered water, heated to 190°F

Combine the brown and white sugars and the vanilla in
a heatproof bowl. Whisk in the hot water until the sugars
have dissolved.

You can store the syrup in the refrigerator for a few weeks.

BOOZY BOBA

Welcome to a whole new way to get your buzz on! We've been putting tea and booze together for fifteen years, since before we even had a boba company. And we've found that the possibilities are nearly endless. Here we're marrying some classic cocktail flavors and techniques with tea to give you a sense of where you can take it—with chewable toppings, of course.

MANGO PASSION FRUIT GREEN TEA HEINEKEN

We want to give credit to our friend Elton Keung, from Labobatory, the king of alcoholic boba. Elton came up at the same time as we did, and you should check out Labobatory. He's also a great hobbyist magician (!), and definitely quite the magician with boozy boba.

In college, we used to play around with making our own alcoholic boba, just by mixing in Kahlúa and Baileys. But Elton took it much further than that, and in the time since, tea cocktails have taken off and we feel like Elton should get more credit for all he contributed to that movement.

One of our favorite drinks of his is a Green Tea Heineken, which boosts the vegetal tea flavors with some deeper, bitter notes from the hops, some carbonation, and a little sweetness. In our homage, we're adding the tropical flavors of mango and passion fruit as well, because it just works, and we're California boys, after all.

MAKES 1 GLASS

RECOMMENDED TOPPINGS: ALCOHOL-INFUSED BOBA (WHITE RUM)

2⅔ ounces (⅓ cup) Mango Passion Fruit Puree (recipe follows)

2 to 4 tablespoons toppings of your choice (optional)

5 ounces (by weight) ice cubes

2⅔ ounces (⅓ cup) Iced Jasmine Tea (page 125)

2⅔ ounces (⅓ cup) Heineken beer

In a glass, layer the puree at the bottom. Add the toppings, if using, the ice, and the jasmine tea. Slowly pour the Heineken over the ice. Mix before drinking.

mango passion fruit puree

MAKES ABOUT 3 CUPS

½ cup fresh passion fruit pulp or store-bought passion fruit puree
2 cups cubed fresh mango
1½ cups filtered water
1 cup raw cane sugar, preferably turbinado

In a blender, blend the passion fruit pulp on medium-low speed to separate the seeds from the pulp. Strain the pulp through a fine-mesh strainer into a bowl. Discard the seeds and rinse the blender out with water. (If you're using store-bought puree, no need to do any of this).

Return the strained pulp (or add the store-bought puree) to the blender. Add the cubed mango, the water, and the sugar, and blend until smooth. Store the puree in the refrigerator for up to 1 week.

MATCHA MULE

Vodka spiced up with ginger and lime, served cold and effervescent in a copper cup—a Moscow Mule is irresistible. We watched as the drink became all the rage in San Francisco circa 2013. In spite of its name, the Moscow Mule is hardly Russian—it's an American invention, and its signature flavors of ginger and lime are straight out of the East. So we had a hunch that adding matcha to the mix, and replacing the vodka with sake, would work. It's like the Asian pantry Mule remix, spicy and sweet like the drink you know and love, but with a green tea vegetal kick.

Hopefully you have a soda siphon, like the one made by iSi, which really extracts the flavors wonderfully. If not, using sparkling water also works fine.

MAKES 3 DRINKS

RECOMMENDED TOPPINGS: NONE

1½ teaspoons matcha powder

7 ounces (¾ cup + 2 tablespoons) cold filtered water (if you have a soda siphon), or the same amount of cold sparkling water

1 extremely thin 1½-inch-long slice of peeled fresh ginger

6 ounces (¾ cup) vodka

3 ounces (¼ cup + 2 tablespoons) Meyer (or regular) lemon juice

Ice cubes, as needed

Place the matcha powder in a small bowl and add 2 tablespoons of the filtered water (or sparkling water). Whisk vigorously to make a thin paste. Slowly add the remaining ¾ cup cold water to the matcha and whisk vigorously until any remaining clumps disappear.

If you have a soda siphon: Add the matcha cold brew, ginger, vodka, and lemon juice to a large siphon canister. Close the canister tightly and shake it. Charge the contents three times with CO_2 cartridges, which will quickly infuse the flavors and carbonate the drink. Fill 3 metal mugs or glasses with ice, and fill them with the drink. Serve.

If you do not have a siphon: Mince the ginger and place it in a metal mug or a glass. Add the sparkling matcha cold brew, the vodka, and the lemon juice. Fill each glass with ice and serve.

TEA SOUR

Citrus and egg whites are the basis for most any drink called a "sour." We like using jasmine in this cocktail because it's light and floral, complementing the bite of the citrus nicely. This is basically a take on a pisco sour, which is a South American staple. Both Chile and Peru claim to have invented it, and we're not going to get into that debate! We just wanted to bring something Asian into the Latin sphere, and the floral jasmine flavor works so well. This is great for a summer evening. Lighter cocktails and green tea just make sense together.

MAKES 1 DRINK

RECOMMENDED TOPPINGS: ALCOHOL-INFUSED BOBA (VODKA)

1 egg white

½ ounce (1 tablespoon) fresh lime juice

½ ounce (1 tablespoon) fresh lemon juice

1 ounce (2 tablespoons) House Syrup (see page 27)

5 ounces (by weight) ice cubes

2 ounces (¼ cup) Jasmine-Tea-Infused Pisco (recipe follows)

1 tablespoon toppings of your choice (optional)

Pour the egg white into a cocktail shaker. Add the lime juice, lemon juice, and house syrup. Shake the contents for 10 seconds. Add the ice and shake again vigorously.

Pour the infused pisco into a glass and add the toppings, if using. Using a fine-mesh strainer, strain the contents of the shaker into the spirits glass. Stir before drinking.

---

jasmine-tea-infused pisco

20 jasmine tea pearls (hand-rolled jasmine tea leaves) or 4 tablespoons loose jasmine tea leaves

1 (750 ml) bottle pisco

Place the tea pearls in a 32-ounce jar, and pour the pisco over them. Seal the jar and allow to infuse for 24 hours. Do not refrigerate.

Strain the pisco, discarding the tea pearls, and store the infused pisco in a mason jar, or pour it back into the original bottle. As long as it is strained well (no sediment), the pisco will remain shelf-stable for a year.

BLACK AND TAN

This is like a brown sugar boba that we had in Taiwan. Kuromitsu is one of our favorite syrups; it's an amazing product, made in Japan from a dark brown, almost black sugar and it has a flavor like a light molasses. Here we pair it with a few dashes of soy sauce for depth and salinity. Add the soy sauce carefully—you don't want it to overpower. A "dash" is like the residue that's left on your finger after you stick your finger into a bit of soy sauce. Very little. Kuromitsu is the secret ingredient here. You want that to stand out.

MAKES 1 DRINK

RECOMMENDED TOPPINGS: ALCOHOL-INFUSED BOBA (JAMESON)

1 tablespoon Kuromitsu brown sugar syrup (or use House Syrup, page 27)

2 dashes soy sauce, or to taste

1 (2-inch) ice cube

2 ounces (¼ cup) Japanese whiskey, such as Suntory

4 dashes orange bitters

1 tablespoon toppings of your choice (optional)

1 (4-inch) strip of orange peel

In a rocks glass, combine the Kuromitsu syrup with the soy sauce. Gently place the ice cube into the glass. Gently pour the whiskey over the ice cube. Add the orange bitters. Stir gently for 20 seconds. Add the toppings, if using, and garnish with the orange peel.

CHAMOMILE CHARTREUSE TEA

Sweet potato shochu is a wonderfully neutral spirit, so the Chartreuse comes through clearly in this drink. And then we add olive oil. We know, adding olive oil to a cocktail sounds a little crazy, but it gives it a great mouthfeel you can't get any other way.

MAKES 1 DRINK

Just making sure we are referring to Japanese *shochu* here, not Korean *soju*?

Right! Although soju is also wonderful and you could even substitute it here!

RECOMMENDED TOPPINGS: CENDOL, FRESCA KONJAC JELLY, ALCOHOL-INFUSED BOBA (SOJU OR PLUM WINE)

2 ounces (¼ cup) sweet potato shochu or ½ ounce (1 tablespoon) yellow Chartreuse

3 ounces (6 tablespoons) Chamomile Iced Tea (recipe follows)

5 ounces (by weight) ice cubes

1 to 2 tablespoons toppings of your choice (optional)

1 large strip lemon zest

A few drops extra-virgin olive oil

In a mixing glass, combine the shochu or Chartreuse and the chamomile tea. Add the ice and stir gently for 20 seconds.

Spoon the toppings, if using, into a large red wineglass, and strain the cocktail into the glass

Take the strip of lemon zest, hold it over the drink, and twist it. Rub the zest around the rim of the glass for extra flavor and fragrance.

Garnish the cocktail with a few drops of extra-virgin olive oil.

The Boba Book

chamomile iced tea

MAKES 1 CUP + 2 TABLESPOONS (ENOUGH FOR 3 CHAMOMILE CHARTREUSE TEA COCKTAILS)

2 tablespoons chamomile tea flowers

5 ounces (½ cup + 2 tablespoons) filtered water, heated to 180°F

5 ounces (by weight) ice cubes

Steep the chamomile tea flowers in the hot water for 4 minutes. Put the ice cubes in a glass and strain the tea over the ice. Let the ice melt completely.

COFFEE LIQUEUR MILK TEA

ANDREW: True story: I don't even drink. I get Asian flush and become a cheap date. But I'm super social. In college, I would throw parties and at the end of the night people would leave alcohol at my place. One day we ended up with a bottle of Kahlúa, and my two roommates and I talked about adding it to boba . . . *way* before I ever thought of making boba my career. In this cocktail, we're fulfilling that vision. The Galliano Ristretto, a vanilla-forward coffee liqueur from Italy, makes this a little more grown-up. Mint and nutmeg add a subtle spiciness. And condensed milk just makes things delicious.

MAKES 1 DRINK

RECOMMENDED TOPPINGS: ALCOHOL-INFUSED BOBA (JAMESON), EGG PUDDING

1 ounce (2 tablespoons) dark rum

3 ounces (6 tablespoons) Moroccan Peppermint Tea (recipe follows)

1 ounce (2 tablespoons) sweetened condensed milk

1 to 2 tablespoons toppings of your choice (optional)

5 ounces (by weight) ice cubes

2 tablespoons Galliano Ristretto

Dash of grated nutmeg

1 sprig fresh mint

Combine the rum, peppermint tea, and condensed milk in a cup. Stir gently until the condensed milk is completely mixed in.

Put the toppings, if using, and the ice in a glass. Gently pour the Galliano Ristretto over the ice for a layering effect.

Garnish with a dash of grated nutmeg and the mint sprig.

moroccan peppermint tea

MAKES 9 OUNCES (ENOUGH FOR 3 DRINKS)

1 cup filtered water
2 tablespoons gunpowder green tea leaves
1 sprig fresh peppermint
6 ounces (by weight) ice cubes

In a small pot, bring the water to a boil. Spoon 6 tablespoons of the boiling water into a small bowl, add the tea leaves, and swish the leaves around in the water to rinse them. Drain, and add the rinsed tea leaves to the remaining hot water in the pot (off the heat). Add the mint, and steep for 3 minutes.

Put the ice cubes in a bowl or pitcher and strain the tea over the ice, letting the ice melt fully.

TEA-QUILA SUNRISE

You wouldn't necessarily think that India and Mexico would end up in a glass together, but it happens in this drink. The spiciness of the chai stands up to the sugar and juices, which sweeten and enliven it. This one particularly works great as a mocktail—the tequila adds a little bite, but there's already plenty going on. And if you're making our chai blend for our Chai Latte (page 63) or Coconut Chai Tea (page 148), you probably have everything you need for this one in your kitchen right now.

MAKES 1 DRINK

RECOMMENDED TOPPINGS: SAGO, ALCOHOL-INFUSED BOBA (TEQUILA)

1 ounce (2 tablespoons) Masala Chai Syrup (recipe follows)

1 to 2 tablespoons toppings of your choice (optional)

5 ounces (by weight) ice cubes

2 ounces (¼ cup) tequila blanco

½ ounce (1 tablespoon) fresh lime juice

3 ounces (¼ cup + 2 tablespoons) apple juice

Spoon the Masala Chai Syrup into a glass. Add the toppings, if using, and the ice. Gently pour the tequila, then the lime juice and the apple juice, over the ice for a layering effect between the booze and the juice. Stir before drinking.

masala chai syrup

MAKES ABOUT 1¼ CUPS

1 cup filtered water

2 tablespoons Chai Tea Blend (page 63) or store-bought masala chai leaves

¾ cup white sugar

In a small pot over high heat, boil the water. Remove the pot from the heat, add the chai blend to the water, and steep for 3 minutes.

Strain the tea into a container, and add the sugar. Stir to dissolve the sugar completely.

Store the syrup in the fridge for up to 2 months.

ILHA FORMOSA SPIKED TEA

A spiked honey syrup is the foundation of this drink. Our black tea blend plus pink peppercorns make it kind of "fire and ice." It's herbaceous with the thyme, but then there is fresh fruit, too. There's a ton going on in this drink, so we decided to name it for Taiwan, once named the Republic of Formosa, that beautiful island that's the birthplace of boba.

MAKES 1 DRINK

RECOMMENDED TOPPINGS: ALCOHOL-INFUSED BOBA (VODKA)

4 ounces (½ cup) Brewed Boba Guys' Black Tea (page 27)

1 sprig fresh thyme

2 to 3 tablespoons honey

5 pink peppercorns

1 long strip lemon zest

1 to 2 tablespoons toppings of your choice (optional)

5 ounces (by weight) ice cubes

2 ounces (¼ cup) vodka (or any other clear spirit)

5 slices fresh peach

1 small sprig fresh basil

In a small saucepan, combine the black tea, thyme sprig, honey, peppercorns, and lemon zest. Bring the mixture to a simmer over low heat, cover the pan, and simmer for 10 minutes. Remove from the heat. Allow to cool. Strain the tea, discarding the solids.

Put the toppings, if using, in a glass, and add the ice. Pour the spiced tea over the ice. Add the vodka. Garnish with the peach slices and sprig of basil.

SEX ON THE BOBA

With this name, I think there's a good ball joke in here.

We promised Francis we'd keep this PG-13.

Honestly, sex on the boba sounds fun.

Richard has left the chat

This is a straight-up riff on that (in)famous cocktail "Sex on the Beach." We swap plum wine for the schnapps. And we use rooibos, a super-earthy African tea that pairs beautifully with fruit.

MAKES 1 DRINK

RECOMMENDED TOPPINGS: ALCOHOL-INFUSED BOBA (SAKE, PLUM WINE), CENDOL

5 fresh raspberries

1 sprig fresh mint

1 ounce (2 tablespoons) sake (we love Honjozo, higher proof)

1 ounce (2 tablespoons) Japanese plum wine (*umeshu*)

4 ounces (½ cup) Rooibos Iced Tea (recipe follows)

1 ounce (2 tablespoons) honey

1 to 2 tablespoons toppings of your choice (optional)

5 ounces (by weight) ice cubes

In a collins glass, smash the raspberries and mint with a muddler or a spoon. Add the sake, plum wine, rooibos, and honey to the glass. Stir gently until the honey is dissolved and fully incorporated. Add the toppings, if using, and then the ice, and serve.

---

rooibos iced tea

MAKES OVER 1 CUP (ENOUGH FOR 2 COCKTAILS)

2 tablespoons rooibos tea leaves

½ cup + 2 tablespoons filtered water, heated to 180°F

5 ounces (by weight) ice cubes

Add the rooibos to the hot water, and let it steep for 4 minutes.

Put the ice cubes in a pitcher, strain the tea over the ice, and let the ice melt completely.

ELDERFLOWER TEA COCKTAIL

> I actually didn't know what elderflower was until I was shopping at IKEA in my twenties.

> Nothing like getting a bottle of elderflower syrup along with your Ektorp couch!

> And don't sleep on the meatballs.

> You can always get a decent meal at Ikea.

People think of juniper as the flavoring in gin, but many gin blends include sweet elderflower, so we figured, why not do it in a tea and work with that in a cocktail? You might not think condensed milk would work here, with a delicate floral ingredient like elderflower, but it just does. Is there anything condensed milk can't do?

MAKES 1 DRINK

RECOMMENDED TOPPINGS: ALCOHOL-INFUSED BOBA (GIN)

3 ounces (¼ cup + 2 tablespoons) Elderflower Iced Tea (recipe follows)

1 ounce (2 tablespoons) gin (use a really floral one, such as St. George Botanivore or Hendrick's)

½ ounce (1 tablespoon) fresh lemon juice

½ ounce (1 tablespoon) sweetened condensed milk

3 ounces (¼ cup + 2 tablespoons) chilled sparkling wine

1 to 2 tablespoons toppings of your choice (optional)

5 ounces (by weight) ice cubes (optional)

Several edible flowers such as borage, or 1 sprig fresh rosemary, or 1 sprig fresh thyme

Combine the tea, gin, lemon juice, and condensed milk in a cocktail shaker. Shake vigorously for 10 seconds. Strain the drink into a large red wineglass. Top off the glass with the sparkling wine, the toppings, if using, and ice, if desired. Garnish with the edible flowers or herb sprig.

elderflower iced tea

MAKES OVER 1 CUP (ENOUGH FOR 3 COCKTAILS)

2 tablespoons dried elderberry blossoms (elderflowers)

½ cup + 2 tablespoons filtered water, heated to 180°F

5 ounces (by weight) ice cubes

Add the elderflower blossoms to the hot water and steep for 4 minutes.

Put the ice cubes in a glass and strain the tea over the ice. Let the ice melt completely.

ADD-ONS & TOPPINGS

The main thesis of this book is that you can chew your drink. But *what* are you chewing? We have standbys and special toppings at our stores, but in the universe of Asian drinks and desserts, the world of toppings is *massive*. We could have written an entire book just on toppings! So consider this a useful and delicious but by no means comprehensive collection of go-tos when it comes to chewing your drink.

How to Pair Toppings with Drinks

Throughout this book, we've recommended a few toppings with nearly every drink recipe, but feel free to riff and remix however you choose! Here's how we think about toppings overall at Boba Guys: Generally, everything's good with boba—except, for some reason, sparkling drinks. Creamy drinks are best with heavier toppings like almond jelly, black sticky rice, and puddings. Fruity drinks are better with konjac, sago, and lighter things that don't contain dairy or nut milk. Tropical drinks are good with almost anything! So have fun and experiment—that's what we do!

The Feeling of QQ

The outside of the boba ball should be almost like Jell-O. A little soft and smooth, but with a defined exterior and a little film of syrup. When you bite into it, there should be a good bounce to it, like a warm gummy bear. If there's a hard center, that would mean it's undercooked. Too slimy and smooshy, it's overcooked. It should kinda feel like how getting slimed in *Ghostbusters* looks. But, you know, fun and delicious.

Boba Buying Guide

In the early days, we always bought our boba online. (Now we make our own at the US Boba Company, but sorry, we don't sell it retail . . . yet.) Bossen and Lollicup (Tea Zone) are the best names to look for for boba imported from Taiwan. There's also Fanale Drinks (who, full disclosure, is our business partner at US Boba Company). You can buy from all these sources online. With a 6-pound bag of boba, you'll get 64 servings, which is more than enough to get you going. You can also look for these brands at your local Asian specialty store, like 99 Ranch Market. Do *not* buy boba marked "quick cook," "instant," or "5-minute"—the starch that it's made out of is poor quality and the boba hardens very quickly as it cools. Not cute, or QQ.

TAPIOCA BALLS, AKA BOBA

So here they are: the balls that gave us our name. The goal here is to get them to be QQ—the Taiwanese term for chewiness that's similar to the Italian concept of *al dente* . . . but even chewier. The way you control the texture is through the boiling time. Don't use boba that's labeled "quick cook"—that kind of boba has a hardening quality in the starch that isn't properly QQ. We want straight-up tapioca for this recipe. (See Boba Buying Guide on page 185.)

Remember to stir throughout the cooking process. Don't let the boba stick to the bottom of the pot, since that might cause some of the balls to burn or scorch.

The next key is the syrup bath, which adds the flavor. Some places keep their boba in a syrup bath over heat, which is a personal preference. We like our boba to be at room temperature for our drinks. This is for convenience (no need to keep a slow cooker in every store) and also, more important, so it doesn't melt the ice in our drinks and thus dilute the flavors of the ingredients and toppings.

Note that boba is not hard to make right, but it does need to be fairly fresh; we don't hold our boba for more than 4 hours after they're made. After that, they start to turn mushy—very *not* QQ!!

MAKES 4 TO 6 SERVINGS

4 cups filtered water, plus more as needed

1 cup dried boba balls (see Boba Buying Guide, page 185)

½ cup House Syrup (page 27)

In a medium saucepan, bring the water to a rolling boil over high heat. Add the boba and cook for 30 minutes, stirring frequently during the first 10 minutes of cooking to prevent the boba from sitting at the bottom of the pot and burning. Cover the pot so the water doesn't evaporate, and stir occasionally for the remainder of the time. Add more hot water if necessary to keep the boba covered. After the 30 minutes of cooking, take the pot off the heat and let the boba rest for another 30 minutes. After the resting time, strain the boba in a colander or a strainer, discarding the water, and pour them into a mixing bowl. Stir in the syrup. After an additional 30 minutes (so 1½ hours total from the time you started cooking), the boba should have absorbed the sweetness; it won't get any sweeter if it continues to sit longer.

Now your boba is ready to serve; hold it warm or at room temperature (our preference). When you add it to drinks, scoop some of the balls out with a little strainer to leave the syrup behind. The boba keeps for about 4 hours before it starts to lose its texture.

BOOZY BOBA SYRUP

This comes from the days when we were working with our friends at Frozen Kuhsterd, a food truck, back when we were a pop-up. We used to all do a shot together before service. One day, our friend Jason dumped a whole bottle of Jameson in the pot with the boba. Credit to Jason. It was damn good.

Follow the method for Tapioca Balls (opposite), substituting Boozy Syrup for the House Syrup. Serve this to adults only! You'll have extra syrup, which you can save for future boozy boba adventures or mix into your own cocktails in place of simple syrup.

So am I spiking the boba to get a buzz?

Nah, you're just adding flavor, not trying to knock someone out.

MAKES ABOUT 2 CUPS

1 cup dark brown sugar, packed

1 cup white sugar

½ cup filtered water, heated to 190°F

½ cup spirit of your choice (see note)

Combine the brown and white sugars in a heatproof bowl. Whisk in the hot water, stirring until the sugars have dissolved. Slowly whisk in the spirit. Store the syrup in a mason jar or other airtight container. It'll keep indefinitely in the fridge.

NOTE:

We recommend darker spirits like whiskeys or rums, because they're generally sweeter, but you can use any spirit you like to enhance the flavor profile of the drink you're working with. Have fun!

Tapioca Balls, aka Boba
(page 186)

Black Sticky Rice
(page 190)

Grass Jelly
(page 191)

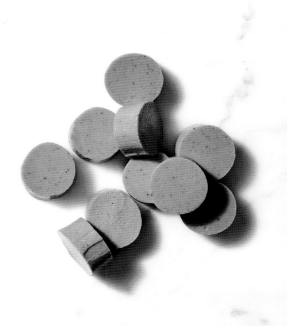

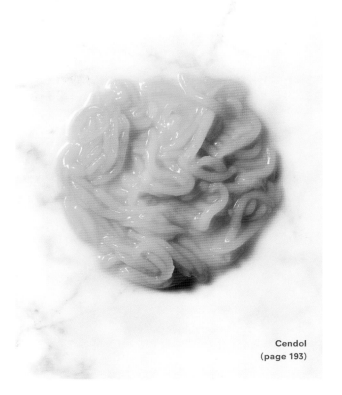

Matcha Pudding
(page 192)

Cendol
(page 193)

Japanese Coffee Jelly
(page 195)

Fresca Konjac Jelly
(page 194)

BLACK STICKY RICE

There's a place called Cha Express in San Mateo that friends of ours run. It's known for its black sticky rice. It's soaked in coconut milk, it's super sticky, and in a drink, it almost turns it into a dessert soup. It doesn't add a huge flavor punch, but the texture is brilliantly chewy, and it can fit in well with lots of different flavors, especially creamy drinks. You wouldn't put this in an agua fresca, for example, but in a horchata? YES.

When the rice is done, it should be a little like oatmeal. You don't want too much water in there—it should be a little slimy (in a good way!). It should hang together and slide slowly off a spoon.

MAKES 12 TO 16 SERVINGS

½ cup black sticky rice

3 cups water

Pinch of salt

½ cup + 2 tablespoons unsweetened coconut milk

½ cup white sugar

In a medium-size saucepan, combine the rice, water, and salt. Bring to a boil over medium-high heat. Then turn the heat to low, cover the pan, and let it cook for 45 minutes.

Add the coconut milk and sugar. Mix everything thoroughly and continue to cook for 30 minutes, covered, stirring occasionally. The rice should be thick and chewy. Remove the saucepan from the heat and allow the rice to cool before serving.

Store the rice in an airtight container, and refrigerate it if not using it within a few hours. It keeps in the fridge for up to 5 days, but it will harden when cold. Microwave it in short bursts to warm it back up to a soft state—or reheat it in a double boiler—before serving.

GRASS JELLY

This is one of our favorite desserts. Some people say grass jelly has a subtle licorice flavor. To us, it can kind of tastes like a Ricola cough drop, but dialed way back and without all that sinus-clearing menthol. It's mellow, smooth, herbal, and refreshing. Andrew's grandmother made this at home and Bin remembers it from before he left Taiwan as a kid. It's a classic dessert—just add honey or condensed milk.

The "grass" comes from a plant—Chinese mesona—that's part of the mint family. The leaves are boiled to make an extract. We add gelatin and cornstarch to give it structure. Chinese mesona is used for many medicinal purposes; it's high in potassium and is said to be anti-diabetes, anti-cancer, anti-diarrhea, and good for digestion. So it's a win-win. You can make it into a delicious dessert, and your grandma thinks it will make you live forever.

> Sounds like the Asian chia seed!

> Did you also go through a hot yoga phase?

> LOL, yes. But I did not wear those little shorts.

> You learn so much about somebody when you write a cookbook together!

MAKES ABOUT 12 SERVINGS

1 tablespoon gelatin powder

1 cup + 6 tablespoons cold filtered water

1 tablespoon cornstarch

2 tablespoons white sugar

1 tablespoon honey

1 cup liquid grass jelly extract (you should be able to find this at an Asian market like 99 Ranch Market or online)

In a large heatproof container (larger than a quart), sprinkle the gelatin over 6 tablespoons of the cold water. Set aside for 5 minutes to let the gelatin bloom.

In a small cup, thoroughly mix together ¼ cup of the remaining water and the cornstarch.

In a small saucepan, combine the remaining ¾ cup water with the sugar, honey, and liquid grass jelly extract. Cook over high heat, stirring occasionally, until the contents reach 180°F (use a thermometer). Stir in the cornstarch mixture and cook, stirring, for a minute or two, until the mixture thickens and turns clear.

Pour the hot grass jelly mixture into the bloomed gelatin and stir until the gelatin fully dissolves. Pour the mixture into a wide, shallow container. Allow it to cool and then store it in the fridge for at least 12 hours before serving.

Cut the jelly into ½- or ¼-inch dice for use in drinks, or in larger dice to serve as a dessert.

Store the grass jelly in the fridge for up to a week.

MATCHA PUDDING

Matcha drinks and matcha-flavored sweets have become a thing in the U.S. recently, but when you visit the origins of modern matcha—Japan—you really see what full-on matcha love looks like. It's a borderline obsession for many.

A lot of people cite Tokyo as their Japanese foodie destination, but Kyoto wins when it comes to matcha, no contest. Kyoto is near Uji, a town of tea farms that is famous for its matcha production. Walk around Kyoto and you'll see Uji matcha dessert shops everywhere. And they're all good.

We can probably make a whole book about matcha desserts, but this pudding recipe should give you a small taste. We went for balance in our recipe as we cater to the American palate, so it's less bitter and grassy than in Japan, but just as enjoyable.

MAKES 8 TO 12 SERVINGS

2 cups whole milk

1 tablespoon gelatin powder

½ cup white sugar

3 large egg whites

½ teaspoon salt

2 tablespoons matcha powder

Pour 1 cup of the milk into a medium-size heatproof container. Sprinkle the gelatin over it and allow it to sit for 10 minutes.

Meanwhile, in a mixing bowl, whisk together the sugar, egg whites, salt, and matcha powder until the mixture is fully combined and is starting to foam. Strain it through a mesh strainer into a bowl.

In a small pot, place the remaining 1 cup milk over medium heat. Immediately add the egg white mixture to the milk and cook, stirring, until it reaches 180°F. (Use a candy thermometer.)

Immediately pour the contents of the pot into the bloomed gelatin. Mix thoroughly until the gelatin is fully dissolved. Pour the mixture into a shallow baking dish or flat container, and allow it to set overnight in the refrigerator to solidify.

Cut the pudding into ¼- to ½-inch cubes before serving. Store it in the fridge for up to 1 week.

CENDOL

Any Southeast Asian (and especially Malaysians, Singaporeans, and Indonesians) will know—and most likely have an undying love for, nostalgia about, or at least indelible lasting memories of—cendol. It's pronounced CHEN-dol, and it's a little like how nostalgic Jell-O is to generations of people in the U.S.

Cendol is almost like stretched-out boba with extra punches of flavor and color. When you make it right, it looks a little like bright green gummy worms. Pandan leaves traditionally give it its green tint, and they add a bold nutty/grassy/vanilla flavor. It's a flavor that's hard to describe but iconic and amazing. Try it!

MAKES 8 TO 12 SERVINGS

¼ cup tapioca starch
¼ cup sweet rice flour
2 teaspoons pandan extract
½ teaspoon salt
2 tablespoons white sugar
1½ cups water

In a mixing bowl, combine the tapioca starch, sweet rice flour, pandan extract, salt, sugar, and water. Mix the ingredients thoroughly until they form a smooth, thin paste.

Fill a large mixing bowl with ice water.

Transfer the paste to a small saucepan and cook it over low heat, stirring occasionally, until it bubbles and thickens into a sticky batter and turns almost translucent. Set a colander over the bowl of ice water, and use a spoon or a rubber spatula to push small amounts of the batter through the colander holes into the ice water, forming strand-like "noodles."

Allow the cendol to cool for a minute in the ice water, then drain it. Transfer the cendol to a container and add cool water to cover (to prevent clumping). Keep the cendol in the fridge, submerged in water, for up to 3 days.

FRESCA KONJAC JELLY

Konjac is a plant with a tuber that is almost like a sponge in texture and appearance. You may have seen packages of gluten-free, fat-free, grain-free, almost calorie-free noodles called shirataki. Well, they're made out of konjac. When you rehydrate konjac powder, it creates a bouncy, chewy kind of starch that is all texture. It doesn't add a ton of flavor. But that means it can let the flavor of whatever you set with it really come through; for example, with our tea frescas. You can even have a suspended effect of the fruit hanging in the jelly, which looks really nice. For that, allow the hot mixture to cool to room temperature. It should start to thicken. At that point, sprinkle in the fruit gingerly, so some pieces don't sink all the way to the bottom, and complete the cooling process.

You can find konjac jelly powder in Asian supermarkets like 99 Ranch Market, or online.

MAKES 12 TO 16 SERVINGS

2 cups Strawberry Jasmine Tea Fresca (page 124) or Mango Matcha Fresca (page 127)

2 tablespoons konjac jelly powder

1 cup chopped fresh strawberries

Combine the tea fresca and the konjac jelly powder in a medium-size saucepan and bring to a boil over high heat, stirring so it doesn't stick. Allow the powder to fully dissolve, boiling it for about 5 minutes. Then remove the pan from the heat and let it cool.

Pour the mixture into a flat, shallow container and add the chopped strawberries, stirring to distribute them evenly. Set the mixture aside to cool.

Refrigerate the cooled mixture for at least 3 hours, until set, before serving. Cut it into ¼- or ½-inch cubes and serve. Store it in the fridge for up to 1 week.

JAPANESE COFFEE JELLY

Coffee jelly is all over Japan, and we love it. Great sweetened coffee in a gelatin form—what's *not* to love? Any milk-based (or milk-alternative-based) drink would be great with this, and it's also a fun topping to dress up a scoop of vanilla ice cream.

MAKES 8 TO 12 SERVINGS

2 cups Cold Brew Coffee (page 151)

2 tablespoons gelatin powder

¼ cup filtered water

¼ cup white sugar

In flat, shallow heatproof container, combine ¼ cup of the cold brew with the gelatin. Bloom (soak) the gelatin for at least 5 minutes.

In a small saucepan, bring the water to a boil over high heat, and add the sugar. Allow the water to come back up to a boil. Pour the boiling sugar water over the bloomed gelatin and mix until the gelatin is fully dissolved. (If the gelatin does not fully dissolve, pour it all into the saucepan and cook over medium-high heat until any visible clumps are gone; then return it to the container.) Add the remaining 1¾ cups cold brew. Mix. Store the jelly in the refrigerator to set overnight.

Cut the jelly into ¼- to ½-inch cubes before serving. Store it in the fridge for up to 1 week.

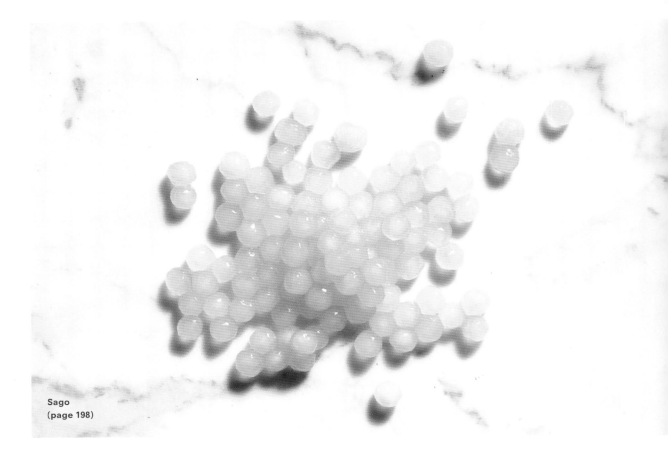

Sago
(page 198)

Coconut Almond Jelly
(page 199)

Tapioca Chia Seed Pudding
(page 200)

Egg Pudding
(page 201)

Chè Ba Màu Jelly
(page 202)

Mango Pudding
(page 203)

SAGO

In many places, sago is more popular than boba. They're tiny pearls, like mini-boba, but they have a subtler texture: much more tender, silkier, and less bouncy. (They're made from the sago palm, an entirely different starch than tapioca.)

MAKES 8 TO 10 SERVINGS

2 cups filtered water

½ cup uncooked sago pearls (available in Asian markets or online)

In a medium-size saucepan, bring the water to a boil over high heat. Add the sago pearls, bring the water back to a boil, and then lower it to a simmer. Cook for 10 minutes, stirring gently every couple of minutes to prevent clumping and to make sure the pearls aren't sticking to the bottom of the pan. Remove the pan from the heat, cover it, and allow the sago to rest for 10 minutes. Then strain the cooked sago pearls and rinse them under cold running water.

Store the sago in a container with enough water to cover until you're ready to use them. To serve, strain out the pearls to add them to drinks. Sago will keep in an airtight container in the fridge for up to 3 days.

COCONUT ALMOND JELLY

In Western cooking, jellies are usually reserved for fruit or lean flavors, but in Cantonese desserts, you often see jellies made from rich nuts or seeds, like almond or sesame. Almond jelly is common in the cafés of Hong Kong, or in really old-school British Hong Kong fruit cocktails. Here we make it with coconut to add a richer spin. It's set with agar, a plant-based gelatin-like powder that creates a jelly that's tender but with a firmer structure, unlike the meltiness of gelatin-based jellies.

This works really well with strong-flavored citrus drinks or anything with grapes—or most fruits, really—by providing a nutty, round, mellow flavor to go with that sweet-tart punch.

You can also eat this on its own. We have a certain subset of customers who order a drink with the almond jelly on the side, and ask for a spoon. We don't judge!

MAKES 12 TO 16 SERVINGS

1 cup water

1 cup white sugar

1 tablespoon agar powder

1¼ cups unsweetened coconut cream

½ tablespoon almond extract

2 cups whole milk

In a medium saucepan, bring the water to a boil over high heat. Add the sugar and agar to the boiling water and whisk together until dissolved. Turn the heat down to medium, add the coconut cream and almond extract, and cook for 2 to 3 minutes, until the mixture has a thick milky consistency.

Take the pan off the heat and thoroughly mix in the whole milk. This will bring the temperature down and allow the jelly to set more quickly. Pour the mixture into a shallow baking dish or shallow bowl and allow it to set in the fridge for at least an hour before serving.

Cut the jelly into ¼- or ½-inch dice for drinks. Store it in the fridge for up to a week.

TAPIOCA CHIA SEED PUDDING

There's no other way we can think of to say this: this is the whitest Asian thing we've ever made. Andrew's wife, Kelly, is a big yogi and loves eating healthy. She and her friends fell in love with chia, which is having a huge moment in the U.S. for its health benefits and its appetite-suppressing qualities.

It's a cool ingredient, no doubt, in that it can sort of gel liquids and turn them into "puddings" all by itself. But we love adding tapioca pearls to the chia pudding. Not boba—we mean those little tapioca pearls you find in Western tapioca pudding. It switches up the texture with the tiny chia seeds, which give a little crunch and pop to the tender chew of the tapioca. It's like Taipei meets Venice Beach. That's bridging cultures!

MAKES 8 TO 12 SERVINGS

½ cup small tapioca pearls (not boba, and not sago, but the tiny pearls you see in mass-produced tapioca pudding)

2 cups filtered water

¼ cup chia seeds

3 cups almond milk or light unsweetened coconut milk

½ teaspoon salt

¼ cup white sugar

Put the tapioca pearls in a medium-size bowl and add the water. In an airtight storage container, combine the chia seeds with 1½ cups of the almond or coconut milk. Refrigerate the tapioca mixture and the chia mixture overnight.

Strain the tapioca and discard the water.

In a medium-size saucepan, combine the remaining 1½ cups almond or coconut milk with the salt and sugar and bring it to a boil over high heat, stirring occasionally to prevent burning. Turn the heat to low and add the tapioca. Simmer, stirring occasionally to prevent sticking, for 30 to 45 minutes, until the tapioca is plump and translucent. Take the pan off the heat and allow it to cool for 10 minutes, stirring occasionally. Then add the soaked chia seeds to the tapioca pudding and mix thoroughly.

Once it has cooled, chill the pudding in the refrigerator. Serve it within 3 days.

EGG PUDDING

You might be familiar with the classic, "dan tat," Hong Kong egg tart, with a filling almost like flan. That filling has morphed into a topping for drinks—one of our comfort foods.

The directions here are for the stovetop, for which you'll want a candy thermometer to monitor the temperature. You can also sous vide this, if you're into that. Just set your immersion circulator to 180°F and follow this same process. (That's actually how we make it in bulk.)

MAKES 12 TO 16 SERVINGS

3 cups whole milk

1½ tablespoons gelatin powder

3 large egg yolks

¾ cup white sugar

1 tablespoon vanilla extract

Pour 1 cup of the whole milk into a lidded heatproof container that is large enough that you can use a whisk to mix its contents but small enough that it can fit inside a large stockpot. Sprinkle the gelatin over the milk and refrigerate it for 10 minutes to allow the gelatin to bloom.

In a mixing bowl, whisk together the egg yolks, sugar, vanilla extract, and the remaining 2 cups milk. Take the gelatin mixture out of the fridge and add the yolk mixture to it. Cover the container tightly with plastic wrap and put the lid on.

In a large stockpot, add enough water to submerge the container of egg pudding. Bring the water to 180°F over high heat, then turn the heat down to maintain that temperature. Submerge the egg pudding container in the hot water and cook, keeping an eye on the temperature of the water so it doesn't go above 180°F, until the egg mixture has an internal temperature of 180°F, about 30 minutes. The point is to heat all the ingredients to a safe temperature.

Once the egg mixture hits 180°F, remove the container from the heat, remove the lid and the plastic wrap, and whisk the contents together. The egg mixture will still be liquid at this point. Now it's time to let it cool and give the gelatin a chance to set. Put the lid back on and refrigerate the pudding for at least 12 hours to solidify. (If you have the space in your fridge, pour the mixture into a wide, shallow pan and let it set in that; it'll make dicing it a bit easier later.)

You can store the egg pudding in the fridge for up to 1 week. Cut the pudding into ¼- to ½-inch cubes before serving.

CHÈ BA MÀU JELLY

This tricolored Vietnamese confection (its name literally means "three-color dessert") is a drink and a dessert on its own. Coconut milk provides the base, topped with jackfruit, red beans, and a coconut milk jelly, usually presented in layers. It's one of the OG chewable drinks. You see this a lot in Vietnamese restaurants, and we love it after a bowl of phở.

Like boba, many variations are possible here. You can use different beans, layer differently, swap out the jackfruit for something else, and so on. But this basic recipe will give you the baseline for any experiments.

We've refashioned this classic into a topping by turning chè ba màu's components into a single dice-able jelly that you can add to drinks.

MAKES 12 TO 16 SERVINGS

1½ cups unsweetened coconut milk

½ cup white sugar

½ tablespoon agar powder

1 cup Cendol (page 193)

½ cup canned red kidney beans, drained

1 cup finely chopped jackfruit (fresh or thawed from frozen)

Pour the coconut milk into a medium-size saucepan and cook over medium heat until it is warm (you don't need to boil it; you're just heating it up to dissolve the sugar). Add the sugar and agar powder. Slowly whisk it all together until everything has dissolved. Remove the saucepan from the heat and pour the mixture into a container. Allow this to cool on the countertop for at least 10 minutes, until it is just warm to the touch.

In a large shallow baking dish or other container, combine the cendol, kidney beans, and jackfruit; spread the mixture out in an even layer. Pour the coconut milk mixture over this, making sure it's covering all the bits. Store in the fridge for 3 hours or until set.

Cut the jelly into ¼- to ½-inch cubes before serving. Store it in the fridge for up to 1 week.

MANGO PUDDING

You might have seen heart-shaped dishes of golden-orange mango pudding at Cantonese-style dim sum restaurants, being wheeled by on carts along with the egg custard tarts and bowls of soft tofu.

We're making our own version of that dessert and cutting it up into cubes for a topping.

MAKES 12 TO 16 SERVINGS

1½ cups filtered water

¼ cup gelatin powder

1 pound diced mango, thawed if frozen

1¼ cups white sugar

¾ cup heavy whipping cream

¼ cup whole milk

Pour ½ cup of the water into a large heatproof mixing bowl. Sprinkle the gelatin over the surface and let it sit for 10 minutes.

Put the mangoes, sugar, cream, and milk in a blender. Blend on medium-low speed until smooth. Pour the puree through a fine-mesh strainer into a bowl, using a rubber spatula to push the mixture through the strainer. Discard any pulp left over in the strainer.

In a small saucepan, warm the remaining 1 cup water over high heat until it starts to boil. Pour the water over the bloomed gelatin in the mixing bowl. Mix until all the gelatin is dissolved. Add the mango mixture and stir until everything is combined. Pour the mixture into a wide, shallow container and let it set for at least 12 hours in the refrigerator before serving.

Cut the pudding into ¼- to ½-inch dice before serving. Store it in an airtight container, refrigerated, for up to 1 week.

Oh yeah, I totally know those little heart-shaped desserts!

Wait, seriously, why are they always heart-shaped??

Sounds like a good topic for my next article for Eater.com!

Please cite your sources.

REFLECTIONS
FROM ASIA

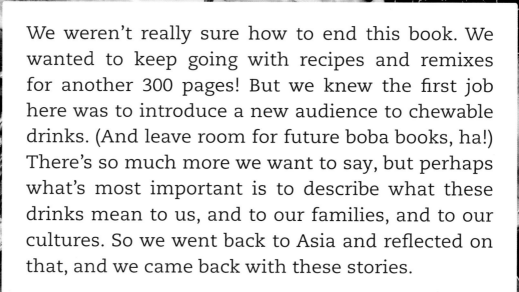

We weren't really sure how to end this book. We wanted to keep going with recipes and remixes for another 300 pages! But we knew the first job here was to introduce a new audience to chewable drinks. (And leave room for future boba books, ha!) There's so much more we want to say, but perhaps what's most important is to describe what these drinks mean to us, and to our families, and to our cultures. So we went back to Asia and reflected on that, and we came back with these stories.

AGŌNG
BY BIN

I'm on a high-speed train barreling through the countryside somewhere between Taipei and Kaohsiung, on my way to visit my grandfather, thinking about Taiwan, and America, and boba, and what it all means. We were in Taiwan to research and shoot for this book on a packed itinerary, but at the last minute I decided I couldn't be this close to my grandfather and not go see him.

This might sound weird to you, but I don't even know my grandfather's name. It's not because we aren't close, or that I don't love him. It's just that, in our culture, personal names aren't as important as terms of respect. I've always just called him 阿公 (agōng), "grandfather."

Agōng speaks only Taiwanese, not even Mandarin. It's a dying language. Agōng is descended from the tribal people of Taiwan. That whole side of my family is darker, taller, with higher cheekbones. Agōng was a farmer all his life. He never learned to read.

When agōng dies, my family's older Taiwanese culture will go with him. The only time anybody speaks Taiwanese in my family—if they know any Taiwanese at all—is with agōng. I have to get my dad or my cousins to translate for me.

My current conversational relationship with agōng can be basically summed up as his asking me, "When are you going to get married?" My grandfather is the last of his generation, but he's also the eldest son. And my father is my grandfather's eldest son, and I'm my father's eldest son. Being the eldest son of the eldest son of the eldest son

is a big deal. All my cousins are younger, and mostly girls. I think about that.

But I worry that if I tell agōng I'm going to get married, he'll figure his legacy will live on and decide to let go of his life. I figure, I'll keep him waiting around to see that happen.

I was born in Taiwan in 1982, in the pre-boba era. But even if there had been boba around when I was living there, I probably wouldn't have tasted it. We had a very simple, modest life with few luxuries, the way agōng lives to this day. Then my parents and I moved to Texas, and agōng stayed on the farm.

When I discovered boba, near where I took Mandarin lessons in Houston, I knew it came from Taiwan, but that's not why I loved it. I just loved it because it was delicious. By the time I reached the bottom of my cup of tea, staring at the tapioca balls gathered at the bottom, I'd think how far away from Taiwan I felt—at least the Taiwan I knew, agōng's Taiwan.

I always spent summers at agōng's house outside of Kaohsiung. Agōng worked hard in the fields all day. He drove a big motorcycle. I remember wanting to be like him, riding my bike through the rice paddy fields.

At night I'd play with my cousins, hide from everybody in a giant rice pot they kept in the kitchen, and sleep in the room next to agōng's on a futon in the hot, humid, non-air-conditioned air.

Each year I went to Taiwan to visit, and when I got back to Texas to start another year of school, I noticed that those trips to the boba shop after Mandarin classes meant something a little different to me. Maybe they did make me feel a little more connected to Taiwan. But if I'm being honest, when we started Boba Guys, I wasn't thinking about my homeland. I just wanted to start a business, a bomb company. I wasn't thinking of agōng.

• • •

As we take the turn off the highway in Kaohsiung and head down the country road past the rice paddies, the memories of those summers come flooding back. I remember every turn through the tiny town. I feel like I'm back on my bike again, racing home for dinner at agōng's.

When we pull up to the squat brick house, agōng appears in the doorway to greet us, wearing a thin white short-sleeved shirt and tropical-patterned shorts, and he's just beaming, like the laughing Buddha, but with tears in his eyes. I can see it's hard for him to walk, so I rush over to him. I'm overcome by emotion, and I don't know what I'm saying to him or what he understands of what I'm saying, but he gives me a big hug. I realize later that Andrew is following me around, filming everything, with tears in his eyes.

Agōng leads us inside to a small room that smells of incense, wafting up from a Buddhist shrine near a TV that's blasting car-

toons. When he sits down, he wipes the tears from his eyes and he tells me it's good to see me. When he speaks, it's with a strong lisp, which he's had since he was a kid. It's actually the reason he never learned to read. A teacher made fun of him, so he left school and never went back; he started working in the fields instead.

Soon the house is filled with aunts and cousins and other friends and relatives, more than a dozen in all, all here to see me—even though I only told them I was coming yesterday. Before long, the plates of food start to come out: boiled duck with sweet sauce, fried duck with ginger and basil, soup, shrimp, bananas and jujubes and grapes grown on my family's farms. I hear stories about my dad when he was a kid, stealing motorcycles and drinking booze, and then we FaceTime my dad briefly back in Texas, where it's the middle of the night, but agōng can't work the iPhone too well, so we say goodbye.

I look up above where I'm sitting—next to my agōng, an illiterate pig farmer who didn't even finish elementary school—to see that the walls are lined with framed photographs of his children graduating from college. And then in the middle of the wall, I see a handmade piece of Boba Guys fan art. It's a photo of me wearing a lab coat, at one of our early pop-ups, pasted to a piece of construction paper that's bedazzled with plastic jewels. I think some of my cousins must have put that together for agōng, who now proudly displays it in his living room. Here I am, his grandson, the successful American businessman.

There isn't a cup of boba in sight. In fact, agōng has still never had boba. But I know he feels the same way I do about it, because boba isn't just boba, after all. It's a symbol of how far we've come as a family. From an illiterate pig farmer to his son, an immigrant engineer in Texas, to his son, the boba king-pin, who's come back triumphantly from San Francisco. In a way, even though he's never seen it, I feel like agōng gave me boba, and I just took it and ran with it.

I don't know how to say this to him—in Taiwanese, Mandarin, or even English. I open my mouth to try, but just at that moment, agōng squints at me, cracks a mischievous grin, and asks me when I'm going to get married, and we all burst into laughter.

C'mon, you going to tell 'em, Bin?

All right, here we go:

Photo by Augie Chang

UNCLE MICHAEL
BY ANDREW

How much of our past continues into our present? How much do we honor the sacred and how much tradition do we keep?

I think about this stuff all the time. I think about my parents. Like many immigrant children, I owe everything to them, from how my dad survived as a Freedom Swimmer escaping Communist China to how he and my mom raised her children in a third culture with no more than a high school diploma.

But this story isn't about my parents. It's still about family though. During our trips to Asia, there was a moment that I shared with Bin and Richard that distills this book down to its cultural concentrate.

I went to my Uncle Michael's apartment in Shanghai to hear stories about my family's past, but I felt like I was staring at the future. I wanted sordid accounts of their struggle to live the American Dream, but I ended up with something more nuanced.

Uncle Michael lives on the forty-sixth floor of the Four Seasons in Pudong, among the cluster of skyscrapers that line the Bund, the famous Shanghai skyline you might recognize from your Apple TV display. It's all mirrors and sleek lines with a million-dollar view. Six hundred feet in the air, you can see all of Shanghai's famous contrasts: the squat old houses and the high-rises, the new and the old, colliding. A drone buzzes along the side of the building.

Ever since I was young, my mom told me to learn from my Uncle Michael. "He's very successful. He never has to worry about money." He grew up poor in China and moved to San Francisco as a teenager. He worked as a dishwasher and eventually he met a banker at his restaurant job. One thing led to the next, and now, like Mufasa, he gets to tell his son Justin, "Everything the light touches . . . is our kingdom."

Uncle Michael works with robotics, sensors, and innovations from the U.S. that he brings to scale in China. He's American-trained, but culturally Chinese, a product of both. Progressive and pragmatic, but respectful of tradition and culture.

His cross-cultural take on business and culture is a huge reason why Boba Guys exists to this day. Nearly a decade ago, I sat in the heart of XinTianDi, a popular expat district in Shanghai, eating Häagen Dazs with him. "If the West can come here, you can do the same. Anything is possible," he said, and boom. The seed of Boba Guys was planted.

More than anyone I know, he embodies the American Dream.

• • •

"Justin!"

Uncle Michael is drinking a nice Burgundy, but since I'm in town and brought company, he wants to give boba a try. My cousin appears from a room where he's probably been playing Fortnite for hours. Justin is born and raised in China, but he seems even more American than I am. Like many Chinese kids, he wants to be a basketball star like Jeremy Lin.

"Justin, go get us some of this . . . boba . . . "

The word pops out of my uncle's mouth somewhat awkwardly. "Dude, just call it, bruh," Justin says to his dad, gesturing at his smartphone.

It takes a while for even the most modern elevator to get forty-six floors down, after all. I think of the country shacks that once lined the Huangpu River below. There's barely a trace of them left. Uncle Michael's life is a little like that. I see little of the poor Chinese kid or the hungry young immigrant dishwasher in the man who's using his smartphone to have drinks delivered to his Jason Bourne–ass apartment.

The boba arrives. After sucking back a few sips and chewing on the boba (his only carbs in weeks, he'll tell us later), my uncle makes a quizzical face. He doesn't seem too impressed. That's OK though—my uncle is hard to impress. That's part of what I like about him. It's part of what makes him successful.

He finally speaks. "Maybe you should invent a new drink."

We tell him boba is a new drink for most of the world. It's why we are interviewing him for the book. We explain that boba drinks are made for endless remixes and creativity. That it tells a story about the past and the future. It's a living allegory for what's happening in the world today.

Uncle Michael looks thoughtful, if dubious. "When your mother told me what you were doing with this company, I asked her, will it be big?"

"You know, I took that as a challenge," I tell him. I look to Bin, who's learned over the years about my Tiger Uncle and extended Tiger Family. "Now we serve ten thousand people every week." I have no idea why I chose to flex. American reflex, I think.

My uncle nods. He doesn't seem blown away, but it's a warm nod. He asks me how profitable our company is. I tell him about our book—this book—and how it's part of our vision to bridge cultures. I find this innate desire to prove my worth to him. I'm now too timid to tell him about our plans for international expansion. But he lights up when I make a flippant joke about how maybe Boba Guys will make Bin or me the first Asian President of the United States. "After all, the Starbucks guy wants to give it a try."

"Good," he says. "I have people to support you." He means it, even as his boba sits on the table in front of him, half-drunk, the ice melting away.

OUR (NEW) AMERICAN (BOBA) DREAM

So where do we fit into all this? And where does boba fit into all of this? (How is such a beautiful recipe book packing in so many truth bombs?)

We spent many a night pondering about what to make of Agōng and Uncle Michael's stories. Originally, we related more to the simple comfort of Agōng, yet we couldn't deny the appeal of chasing bigger dreams.

It finally dawned on us in the eleventh hour of finishing up this book. It's not about trading off the past for the future, tradition or progress. It's not a new chapter we're writing, it's a new book, entirely. We're a new generation, a third culture, and we take inspiration from both role models.

Agōng farmed pigs; we make boba. But we try to do it the way he did it: with hard work, and with the wisdom of tradition. Boba is also a drink that looks at the future, like Uncle Michael does: it's always evolving, remixing, and progressing.

This little boba book was never intended to be a history lesson or handbook on navigating East versus West, but it is a clear metaphor for society today. Beneath the pretty pictures, ingredients, and personal stories is the fundamental belief that culture is organic and fluid.

We asked this question at the beginning of the book, but again: What is boba? It's not static. It's a moving target.

ANDREW: It's true in every form of culture.

RICHARD: Ahem, guys?

BIN: Music, movies, food.

RICHARD: Speaking of which, hey guys?

BIN: Soon there will be a bridge to every culture, and you'll see it in every drink.

ANDREW: There may be some fighting and missteps along the way.

RICHARD: Guys, we gotta wrap up this book.

BIN: But as long as we give attribution where it's due, maybe we can learn to celebrate our differences and move forward together.

ANDREW: And maybe these conversations can help save us from World War III.

RICHARD: CAN'T WE ALL JUST GET OOLONG!?!?

ANDREW: LOL, I can't believe a white guy's going to get the last word in *The Boba Book*, but . . .

BIN: That's the perfect place to end.

EPILOGUE

So we want to officially end this book by dedicating it to the friends, family, fans, and team that supported us throughout this entire journey. The ones who came out to our original pop-up in the Mission. The ones who came to every store's opening. The ones who come hear us speak at conferences and meet-ups. The ones who worked for us and gave us their blood, sweat, and tears (many) as we built this movement and changed an entire industry. This book is a capstone to the first phase of Boba Guys. We wanted to make this book about the world of boba, but we hope we can indulge a bit and talk about the immediate community that directly contributed to our mission. You kept us going when we wanted to give up. When landlords said boba was "too Asian" or "not the crowd we want." Or when the press said boba was unhealthy, too exotic, or look like "blobs." You had our back.

This book is meant to be both a primer and celebration of all things boba, but it's also cultural kindling.

We know a lot of attention goes to things like global street food, fine dining, and distinguished treats like coffee, chocolate, and pastries. Those are often romanticized in food media. They're great, but we know it's time to take a deeper look at our world, yin liao in all its forms. We spend more time in cafés and tea shops than ever before, but beverage trends come from our world now. We hope to ignite a passion for our beloved drinks, so one day a book like this doesn't seem so out of place. Is it an Asian recipe book? Is it an American mocktail book? Neither. It's an Asian-American book on global drink culture. We aren't coming from the margins anymore. Our identity is in the hyphen!

So with that, Boba Guys and Gals, thank you for your support all these years. We still have a lot of work to do. Here's to bridging cultures!

Acknowledgements from the Boba Guys

As any good Asian children would do, we first want to thank our parents—Danny, Nora, JW, Chiou-Lan—for sacrificing everything and letting us dream big, so that we could live the New American Dream.

Thank you to our wives, Kelly and Kathy. You both are the voices of reason and emotional centers that the public doesn't fully get to see. We love you.

Thank you to our founding team, especially Angela, Gordon and Jesse. This whole thing started with us in the back of Ken Ken Ramen and a tiny storefront in the Mission. You held it down for us as we transitioned this experiment into a full-fledged career.

Thank you to our extended team and alumni who gave their blood, sweat, and MANY tears to serve thousands of people every day. We do not take those long shifts, sticky forearms, and matcha stains for granted. You all helped us create this movement. You are the lifeblood of Boba Guys and the true heroes we don't deserve.

Thank you to Eugene "Culture King" Hu, Janet Hsieh, Chris St. Cavish, Laura Lu, Laura Huang, Benjamin Marston, Heyman De Luz, David Fan, Allen and Ayaka Lu, Jia and Mari, and all of our extended global family who gave us an inside look at China, Taiwan, Japan, and greater Asia.

Thank you, Francis Lam, for believing that we were the right people to write the first book on the boba world. Thanks for all the guidance, patience, and Medici-like food wisdom!

Thank you, Kitty Cowles, our Jerry Maguire, our ambassador of "quan." We didn't know an agent could also become a therapist, copywriter, project manager, and life coach.

Thank you, Richard Parks III, for your colorful lens on life. Your curiosity, patience, and empathy made this book so much fun to work on. We really need more projects to work on together so we can travel the world and negotiate in foreign languages.

Thank you Christopher Testani and Anson Smart for making our drinks look next-level. Chris, we hope you can join us again in our next book!

Thank you Jen Wang, Serena Wang, Lydia O'Brien, Stephanie Huntwork, Doris Cooper, Aaron Wehner, and the Clarkson Potter team for making us look good and believing our underrepresented story is something people want to hear.

Thank you, Alex Lam and the Boba Guys Product team, who made all the recipes happen. Shout-outs also to Nora Haron and Carlo Splendorini who generously lent us their particular set of skills to make some of the harder recipes really pop. Also, kisses to sexy chef Deuki Hong for leveling up our culinary game.

Thank you to all the recipe testers: Minji Chang, Shirley Wen, Katie Myrick, Erica Coggio, Amy Wang Hernandez, Ilene Feng, Abby Latip, Rebekah Wong, Vivian Kelly, Sarah Nguyen, Michelle Paitich, Anthony Lum, Georgiana Ng, Joy Tamaki, Stephen Lo, Virginia Yi, Nicole Chiu-Wang, Linette Kim, and Maria

Zizka. Y'all BTS (Boba Test Subject) Army! Who would have thought you can bribe people to test nearly a hundred recipes with free boba?!

Thank you to our mentors who bet on young, scrappy, and hungry entrepreneurs with bold visions. Robert, Stefan, Taka, Dr. Glenn Griffin, Michael Bozalina, Dan Lin, Wen Zhou, Peter Yen, Hanson Li, and Lin-Manuel Miranda (we don't know you but just putting it out there in the universe).

Lastly, thank you to all our friends, fans, supporters, and other boba shops around the world. Your DMs, comments, tweets, and emails fuel us to be better every day. We are so grateful that we have an army to carry out our mission of bridging cultures. We hope to make you proud and bring home a James Beard Award someday . . . or at least a "People Love Us on Yelp" sticker.

Acknowledgements from Richard Parks III

Thank you, Francis Lam, whose soothing baritone *always* made me feel like I was simultaneously on *The Splendid Table*, slowed my heartbeat, and made me believe everything was going to be OK . . . and it was. Thanks also for publishing the mango video in 2009.

Kitty, for whipping this book into shape in the early stages, inviting me into this project in the first place, and also hanging tough and caring about how it all evolved throughout.

Rebecca Friedman, for being not just an agent but a ride-or-die lifetime friend.

BG fam. Especially Alex Lam, wow! You made this cookbook happen, because what's a cookbook without recipes? Thank you for always being available, nights and weekends, and after work. I learned so much.

Thank you to Jen Wang, Serena Wang, Lydia O'Brien, Stephanie Huntwork, the Clarkson Potter leadership—and to all who helped make this book happen.

Testani, you're the pop-art Pat Metheny of food photogs.

Eugene Hu, for dubbing my sartorial style "grifter." It fits.

To Christopher St. Cavish, you are the nerdy, accute-est Shanghai fixer of dreams. I can't wait to eat your dumplings. (Thank you Marc Johnson for connecting us.)

And thank you Andrew and Bin for taking me to Taiwan and China, for blowing my face off with culture, for table top origami field goals and late-night outside onsens in the rain, and for insisting on including me in this book. Can't wait to do it all over again. DON'T PRAY FOR LOVE!

Index

Note: Page numbers in italics indicate photos separate from recipes.

add-ons and toppings, 183–203
  about: buying boba and, 185; overview of, 183; pairing toppings with drinks, 184
  Black Sticky Rice, 188, 190
  Boozy Boba Syrup, 187
  Cendol, 189, 193
  Chè Ba Màu Jelly, 197, 202
  Coconut Almond Jelly, 196, 199
  Egg Pudding, 197, 201
  Fresca Konjac Jelly, 189, 194
  Grass Jelly, 188, 191
  Japanese Coffee Jelly, 189, 195
  Mango Pudding, 197, 203
  Matcha Pudding, 189, 192
  Rock Sugar Syrup, 83
  Sago, 196, 198
  Salted Buttercream Topping, 113
  Tapioca Balls, aka Boba, 186, 188
  Tapioca Chia Seed Pudding, 196, 200
Agōng, reflections on Taiwan, boba and, 207–9
Air Mata Kucing, 80–81
alcohol. See boozy boba
America, history of boba and, 30
American (boba) Dream, new vision, 213
Asia
  about: overview of reflections from, 205
  Andrew's reflections on successful uncle, boba, and future success, 211–13

Bin's reflections on grandfather (Agōng), Taiwan, boba, and more, 207–9
history of boba and, 15–16, 28–29, 31
Avocado Smoothie, 88–89

bananas
  Banana Jam, 95
  Roasted Banana Milk, 94–95
Bantha Milk, 140–41
basic recipes
  Boba Guys' Tea Blend, 26
  Brewed Boba Guys' Tea Blend, 27
  Classic Milk Tea, 24–25
  House Syrup, 27
beans
  Red Bean Latte, 86–87
  Red Bean Puree, 86
beer, in Mango Passion Fruit Green Tea Heineken, 162
berries
  Fresca Konjac Jelly, 189, 194
  Pink Drink, 134–35
  Raspberry Pineapple Tea Fresca, 126
  Sex on the Boba, 178–79
  Strawberry Cali-pico, 128–29
  Strawberry Jasmine Tea, 124–25
  Strawberry Matcha Latte, 104–5
  Strawberry Puree, 105
  Strawberry Raspberry Puree, 135
Black and Tan, 168–69
Black Sesame Latte (and puree), 92–93
Black Sticky Rice, 188, 190
black tea. See also Ceylon tea
  about: 35; how to mix, 34
  Black Tea Syrup, 96
  Boba Guys' Tea Blend, 26
  Brewed Boba Guys' Tea Blend, 27
  Classic Milk Tea, 24–25
  Coffee Tea Mint Mojito, 144–45

Coffee Tea "Plover," 97
  Hong Kong Milk Tea, 54–55
  Ilha Formosa Spiked Tea, 176–77
  Teh Tarik, 56–57
boba
  about: overview of, 7–8
  "boba" meanings, 20
  bridging cultures, 8, 10
  buying guide, 185
  childhood roots of Andrew and Bin, 43–49
  drinks found in boba shops, 23
  history of, 15–16, 28–31
  making it better, 36
  as "pearls," 20
  QQ texture, 7, 184
  recipe for (Tapioca Balls, aka Boba), 186, 188
  this book and, 13, 39
  tools for making, 40–41
  what it is, 7–8, 14–15, 20
Boba Guys company, about, 20, 36–37, 212–13, 214
Boba Guys' Tea Blend, 26
boozy boba, 161–81
  about: overview of, 161; tools for making cocktails, 40–41
  Black and Tan, 168–69
  Chamomile Chartreuse Tea, 170–71
  Coffee Liqueur Milk Tea, 172–73
  Elderflower Tea Cocktail, 180–81
  Ilha Formosa Spiked Tea, 176–77

Mango Passion Fruit Green
Tea Heineken, 162–63
Matcha Mule, 164–65
Sex on the Boba, 178–79
Tea Sour, 166–67
Tea-Quila Sunrise, 174–75
Boozy Boba Syrup, 187
Brewed Boba Guys' Tea Blend,
27
Brewed Lemongrass
Chrysanthemum Tea, 83
Brewed Thai Tea, 59
Brewed Yerba Maté Tea, 153
bridging cultures, 8, 10
buttercream topping, salted, 113
Butterfly Pea aka Bantha Milk,
140–41
Butterfly Pea Tea, 140–41
buying guide, boba, 185

cake teas, about, 23
Cali-pico, strawberry, 128–29
caramel
Caramel Iced Milk, 146–47
Caramel Matcha Latte, 106–9
Pandan Caramel Sauce, 108–9
Cendol, 189, 193
Ceylon tea
Boba Guys' Tea Blend, 26
Butterfly Pea Tea, 141

Chai Tea Blend, 62
Thai Tea Blend, 59
chai
Chai Latte, 63
Chai Tea Blend, 62
Coconut Chai Tea, 146–47
Masala Chai Syrup, 175
Chamango or Watermelon
Chamoy, 130–31
Chamomile Chartreuse Tea,
170–71
Chamomile Iced Tea, 171
Champurrado, iced, 68–69
Chartreuse, in Chamomile
Chartreuse Tea, 170–71
Chau, Andrew, roots and
reminiscences of Bin and,
43–49, 207–13
Chè Ba Màu Jelly, 197, 202
cheese teas, about, 23
Chen, Bin, roots and
reminiscences of Andrew
and, 43–49, 207–13
China, history of boba/tea and,
15–16, 28–31
chocolate, in Iced
Champurrado, 68–69
chrysanthemum and
lemongrass
Brewed Lemongrass

Chrysanthemum Tea, 83
Iced Lemongrass
Chrysanthemum Tea, 82–83
Lemongrass Chrysanthemum
Blend, 83
Chun Shui Tang, 16, 17, 23
citrus
Lemonade, 123
Limeade, 130
Matcha Palmer, 122–23
POG, 70–71
Classic Milk Tea, 24–25
cocktails, tools for making,
40–41. See also boozy boba
coconut
Coconut Almond Jelly, 196, 199
Coconut Chai Tea, 146–47
Coconut Pandan Drink, 78–79
Halo Halo, 84–85
Li Hing Mui Pineapple Mango
Coconut Drink, 132–33
Li Hing Mui Pineapple Mango
Puree, 133
coffee
Coffee Liqueur Milk Tea, 172–73
Coffee Tea Mint Mojito, 144–45
Coffee Tea "Plover," 96–97
Cold Brew Coffee, 151
"Dirty" Horchata, 150–51
Japanese Coffee Cola, 112–13
Japanese Coffee Jelly, 189, 195
Matcha Coffee, 158–59
Vietnamese Egg Coffee, 76–77
Vietnamese Iced Coffee, 72
cola, Japanese coffee, 112–13
Cold Brew Coffee, 151

crème brûlée/cake/cheese teas
about: overview of, 23
Crème Brûlée Matcha Latte,
154–55
Crème Brûlée Sauce, 155
The Culture Map (Meyer), 18
cultures, bridging, 8, 10

"Dirty" Horchata, 150–51
drinks. *See also* boozy boba;
specialty drinks; traditional
drinks; *specific recipes*
found in boba shops, 23
pairing toppings with, 184. *See
also* add-ons and toppings
photographing, 110–11

Earl Grey Tea, in London Fog,
156–57
eggs
Egg Pudding, 197, 201
Vietnamese Egg Coffee, 76–77
Vietnamese Egg Soda, 74–75
Whipped Egg Cream, 77
Elderflower Iced Tea, 180–81
Elderflower Tea Cocktail, 180–81

Europe,
history of
boba and,
29–30

Fermented
Ume (Green
Plum) Syrup,
100
Fresca
Konjac Jelly,
189, 194
fruit. *See also*
marmalade
drinks;
specific fruit
about: herbal
tea, 35; overview of fruit
teas, 23
POG, 70–71

ginger
about: making juice, 56; syrup,
92
other recipes with, 61, 63, 119,

165
Teh Tarik, 56–57
glasses, coating, 55
"gram your drink, 110–11
Grandfather (Agōng), reflections
on Taiwan, boba and, 207–9
Grass Jelly, 188, 191
green plum. *See* plums and
plum powder
green tea. *See also* matcha
about, 34
Mango Passion Fruit Green
Tea Heineken, 162–63
Moroccan Peppermint Tea
with, 173
guava
POG, 70–71
Yuzu Pear Marmalade Tea,
116–17

half-and-half, as recipe default,
24
Halo Halo, 84–85
Hanlin Tea Room, 16, 17, 23
Haw Flakes Tea, 138–39
herbal tea, about, 35. *See
also* chrysanthemum and
lemongrass; Elderflower Iced
Tea
history of boba, 15–16, 28–31
Hong Kong Milk Tea, 54–55
Horchata, 66–67. *See also* "Dirty"
Horchata
House Syrup, 27

ice, "hitting," 105
Iced Champurrado, 68–69
Iced Jasmine Tea, 125
Iced Lemongrass
Chrysanthemum Tea, 82–83
Iced Matcha Latte, 52–53
Iced Pumpkin Tumeric Latte,
142–43
Iced Sweet Potato Latte, 90–91
Iced Tumeric Latte, 60–61
Ilha Formosa Spiked Tea,
176–77

jackfruit, 85, 202
jam
Banana Jam, 95

Spiced Pumpkin Turmeric
Jam, 143
Ube Jam, 137
Japanese Coffee Jelly, 189, 195
jasmine tea
Iced Jasmine Tea, 125
Jasmine-Tea-Infused Pisco,
166
other recipes with, 126, 128–
29, 162–63, 194
Strawberry Jasmine Tea,
124–25
Tea Sour, 166–67
jelly
Chè Ba Màu Jelly, 197, 202
Coconut Almond Jelly, 196,
199
Fresca Konjac Jelly, 189, 194
Grass Jelly, 188, 191
Japanese Coffee Jelly, 189, 195

Kiwi Guava Marmalade Tea,
116–17
konjac jelly, fresca, 194

lattes
about: compared to milk
teas, 23; overview of, 23;
"shakes," "smoothies" and,
87
Caramel Matcha Latte, 106–9
Chai Latte, 63
Crème Brûlée Matcha Latte,
154–55
Iced Matcha Latte, 52–53
Red Bean Latte, 86–87
lemongrass. *See*
chrysanthemum and
lemongrass
lemons. *See* citrus
Li Hing Mui Pineapple Mango
Coconut Drink, 132–33
Li Hing Mui Pineapple Mango
Puree, 133
Limeade, 130
London Fog, 156–57

Macadamia Nut Condensed
Milk, 73
mango
Chamango or Watermelon

Match Cold Brew, 121
Matcha Coffee, 158–59
Matcha Mule, 164–65
Matcha Palmer, 122–23
Matcha Pudding, 189, 192
Sparkling Rose Matcha, 120–21
Strawberry Matcha Latte, 104–5
melon
Air Mata Kucing, 80–81
Chamango or Watermelon Chamoy, 100–101
milk, caramel iced, 146–47
milk, non-dairy
Macadamia Nut Condensed Milk, 73
Roasted Banana Milk, 94–95
milk teas
about: overview of, 23; using half-and-half in, 24
Classic Milk Tea, 24–25
Coffee Liqueur Milk Tea, 172–73
Hong Kong Milk Tea, 54–55
mint
Coffee Tea Mint Mojito, 144–45
Moroccan Peppermint Tea, 173
mojito, coffee tea mint, 144–45
monk fruit, in Air Mata Kucing, 80–81
Moroccan Peppermint Tea, 173
mule, matcha, 164–65

nuts and seeds
Black Sesame Latte, 92–93
Black Sesame Puree, 93
Coconut Almond Jelly, 196, 199
Macadamia Nut Condensed Milk, 73
Tapioca Chia Seed Pudding, 196, 200

oolong tea, about, 34

pandan
about, 78
Coconut Pandan Drink, 78–79
Pandan Caramel Sauce, 108–9
Pandan Jelly, 79
passion fruit

Mango Passion Fruit Green Tea Heineken, 162
Mango Passion Fruit Puree, 163
POG, 70–71
peaches
Peaches and Cream, 114–15
Roasted Peach Marmalade, 115
pears, in Yuzu Pear Marmalade Tea, 118–19
peppermint tea, Moroccan, 173
photographing drinks, 110–11
pineapple
Li Hing Mui Pineapple Mango Coconut Drink, 132–33
Li Hing Mui Pineapple Mango Puree, 133
Raspberry Pineapple Tea Fresca, 126
Pink Drink, 134–35
pisco, jasmine-tea-infused, 166
"Plover," coffee tea, 96–97
plum wine, Sex on the Boba with, 178–79
plums and plum powder
Fermented Ume (Green Plum) Syrup, 100
Ume (Japanese Green Plum) Soda, 98–100
pudding
Egg Pudding, 197, 201

Chamoy, 130–31
Li Hing Mui Pineapple Mango Coconut Drink, 132–33
Li Hing Mui Pineapple Mango Puree, 133
Mango Lassi, 64–65
Mango Matcha Fresca, 127
Mango Passion Fruit Puree, 163
Mango Pudding, 197, 203
Mango Puree, 65
marmalade drinks, 114–19
about: overview of, 114
Kiwi Guava Marmalade Tea, 116–17
Peaches and Cream, 114–15
Roasted Peach Marmalade, 115
Yuzu Pear Marmalade Tea, 118–19
Masala Chai Syrup, 175
matcha
about: "hitting the ice" with, 105; tools for making, 40–41
Caramel Matcha Latte, 106–9
Crème Brûlée Matcha Latte, 154–55
Iced Matcha Latte, 52–53
Mango Matcha Fresca, 127

Mango Pudding, 197, 203
Matcha Pudding, 189, 192
Tapioca Chia Seed Pudding,
    196, 200
pu-erh tea, about, 35
pumpkin
    Iced Pumpkin Turmeric Latte,
        142–43
    Spiced Pumpkin Turmeric
        Jam, 143
purees
    Black Sesame Puree, 93
    Li Hing Mui Pineapple Mango
        Puree, 133
    Mango Passion Fruit Puree, 163
    Mango Puree, 65
    Red Bean Puree, 86
    Roasted Sweet Potato Puree,
        91
    Strawberry Puree, 105
    Strawberry Raspberry Puree,
        135

QQ texture, 7, 184

raspberries. See berries
recipes. See also boozy boba;
    specialty drinks; traditional
    drinks
    half-and-half as default for, 24

tools for making, 40–41
Red Bean Latte (and puree),
    86–87
rice (sticky), black, 188, 190
Roasted Banana Milk, 94–95
Roasted Peach Marmalade, 115
Roasted Sweet Potato Puree, 91
Rock Sugar Syrup, 83
Rooibos Iced Tea, 178
rose matcha, sparkling, 120–21
Rose Syrup, 121

Sago, 196, 198
sake, Sex on the Boba with,
    178–79
Salted Buttercream Topping,
    113
Sex on the Boba, 178–79
smoothies
    about: lattes, "shakes" and, 87
    Avocado Smoothie, 88–89
    Red Bean Puree for, 86
    Ube Halaya Smoothie, 136–37
soda
    Japanese Coffee Cola, 112–13
    Ume (Japanese Green Plum)
        Soda, 98–100
    Vietnamese Egg Soda, 74–75
Sparkling Rose Matcha, 120–21
specialty drinks, 103–59. See
    also marmalade drinks
    about: overview of, 103;

photographing, 110–11;
    pouring and "hitting the
    ice," 105
Butterfly Pea aka Bantha Milk,
    140–41
Caramel Iced Milk, 146–47
Caramel Matcha Latte, 106–9
Chamango or Watermelon
    Chamoy, 130–31
Coconut Chai Tea, 146–47
Coffee Tea Mint Mojito, 144–45
Crème Brûlée Matcha Latte,
    154–55
"Dirty" Horchata, 150–51
Haw Flakes Tea, 138–39
Iced Pumpkin Turmeric Latte,
    142–43
Japanese Coffee Cola, 112–13
Li Hing Mui Pineapple Mango
    Coconut Drink, 132–33
London Fog, 156–57
Mango Matcha Fresca, 127
Matcha Coffee, 158–59
Matcha Palmer, 122–23
Pink Drink, 134–35
Raspberry Pineapple Tea
    Fresca, 126
Soul Maté, 152–53
Sparkling Rose Matcha, 120–21
Strawberry Cali-pico, 128–29
Strawberry Jasmine Tea,
    124–25

Strawberry Matcha Latte, 104–5
Ube Halaya Smoothie, 136–37
spiked tea, 176–77. *See also* boozy boba
sticky rice, black, *188,* 190
Strawberries. *See* berries
sweet potatoes
  about: sweet potato shochu, 170
  Iced Sweet Potato Latte, 90–91
  Roasted Sweet Potato Puree, 91
syrups and sauces
  about: ginger syrup, 92
  Black Tea Syrup, 96
  Boozy Boba Syrup, 187
  Crème Brûlée Sauce, 155
  Fermented Ume (Green Plum) Syrup, 100
  House Syrup, 27
  Masala Chai Syrup, 175
  Pandan Caramel Sauce, 108–9
  Rock Sugar Syrup, 83
  Rose Syrup, 121
  Vanilla Syrup, 159

Taiwan, boba origins and, 8, 15–16, 29
Tang Dynasty, 28
Tapioca Balls, aka Boba, 186, 188. *See also* boba
Tapioca Chia Seed Pudding, 196, 200
Tea Sour, 166–67
Tea-Quila Sunrise, 174–75
teas, crème brûlée/cake/cheese. *See* crème brûlée/cake/cheese teas
teas, traditional
  about: basics of tea plant, 33; black tea, 35; categories of, 34–35; green tea, 34; herbal tea and, 35; oolong tea, 34; overview of, 23; pu-erh tea, 35; tools for making, 40–41; white tea, 34
  Boba Guys' Tea Blend, 26
  Brewed Boba Guys' Tea Blend, 27
Teh Tarik, 56–57

texture of boba (QQ), 7, 184
Thai Iced Tea, 58–59
Thai Tea Blend, 59
tools of the trade, 40–41
toppings. *See* add-ons and toppings
traditional drinks, 51–101
  about: coating your glass, 55; overview and perspective on "traditional," 51
  Air Mata Kucing, 80–81
  Avocado Smoothie, 88–89
  Black Sesame Latte, 92–93
  Brewed Thai Tea, 59
  Chai Latte, 63
  Chai Tea Blend, 62
  Coconut Pandan Drink, 78–79
  Coffee Tea "Plover," 96–97
  Halo Halo, 84–85
  Hong Kong Milk Tea, 54–55
  Horchata, 66–67
  Iced Champurrado, 68–69
  Iced Lemongrass Chrysanthemum Tea, 82–83
  Iced Matcha Latte, 52–53
  Iced Sweet Potato Latte, 90–91
  Iced Turmeric Latte, 60–61
  Mango Lassi, 64–65
  POG, 70–71
  Red Bean Latte, 86–87
  Roasted Banana Milk, 94–95
  Teh Tarik, 56–57
  Thai Iced Tea, 58–59
  Thai Tea Blend, 59
  Turmeric Tea, 61
  Ume (Japanese Green Plum) Soda, 98–100
  Vietnamese Egg Coffee, 76–77
  Vietnamese Egg Soda, 74–75
  Vietnamese Iced Coffee, 72
turmeric
  Iced Pumpkin Turmeric Latte, 142–43
  Iced Turmeric Latte, 60–61
  Spiced Pumpkin Turmeric Jam, 143
  Turmeric Tea, 61

Ube Halaya Smoothie, 136–37
Ube Jam, 137
U.K., history of boba and, 29–31

Ume (Japanese Green Plum) Soda, 98–100
Uncle Michael, success/boba and, 211–13

Vanilla Syrup, 159
Vietnamese Egg Coffee, 76–77
Vietnamese Egg Soda, 74–75
Vietnamese Iced Coffee, 72
vodka
  Ilha Formosa Spiked Tea, 176–77
  Matcha Mule, 164–65

Whipped Egg Cream, 77
whiskey (Japanese), in Black and Tan, 168–69
white tea, about, 34

yerba maté tea, brewed, 153
Yu Ching Wu, 17–18
Yuzu Pear Marmalade Tea, 118–19

Copyright © 2020 by Andrew Chau and Bin Chen

Photographs copyright © 2020 by Christopher Testani
Photographs in "Boozy Boba" chapter
copyright © 2020 by Anson Smart
All other photographs are courtesy of the authors

All rights reserved.
Published in the United States by Clarkson Potter/
Publishers, an imprint of Random House, a division of
Penguin Random House LLC, New York.

clarksonpotter.com

CLARKSON POTTER is a trademark and POTTER with
colophon is a registered trademark of Penguin Random
House LLC.

Library of Congress Cataloging-in-Publication Data
Names: Chau, Andrew, author. | Chen, Bin. | Parks, Richard.
Title: The Boba book / Andrew Chau and Bin Chen with
Richard Parks.
Description: First edition. | New York : Clarkson Potter/
Publishers, 2019.
Identifiers: LCCN 2019020293 | ISBN 9781984824271
(hardcover)
Subjects: LCSH: Cocktails. | Tea. | Herbal teas. | Smoothies
(Beverages) |
   LCGFT: Cookbooks.

Classification: LCC TX951 .C476 2019 | DDC 641.87/4--dc23 LC

ISBN 978-1-9848-2427-1
Ebook ISBN 978-1-9848-2428-8

Printed in Korea

Book design by Jen Wang
Illustrations by Helen Tseng

10 9 8 7 6 5 4 3 2

First Edition